EGOGRAMS

EGOGRAMS

How I See You and You See Me

John M. Dusay, M.D.

Harper & Row, Publishers

New York, Hagerstown, San Francisco, London

A QUICKSILVER BOOK

EGOGRAMS. Copyright © 1977 by John M. Dusay. All rights reserved. Printed in the United States of America. No part of this book may be used or reproduced in any manner whatsoever without written permission except in the case of brief quotations embodied in critical articles and reviews: For information address Harper & Row, Publishers, Inc., 10 East 53rd Street, New York, N.Y. 10022. Published simultaneously in Canada by Fitzhenry & Whiteside Limited, Toronto.

Designed by C. Linda Dingler

Library of Congress Cataloging in Publication Data
Dusay, John M
  Egograms.
  "A Quicksilver book."
  Includes bibliographical references and index.
  1. Transactional analysis. 2. Self-perception. 3. Ego (Psychology) I. Title.
RC489.T7D87   1977   158   76-62947
ISBN 0-06-062111-7

78 79 80 10 98 76 5 4 3 2

To Katherine:

Whose warm, brilliant, and joyous spirit has contributed so much to this work and to my life.

Contents

Foreword   ix

Important Words   xii

Introduction: Evolution of Egograms   xiii

PART ONE: PRINCIPLES OF EGOGRAMS   1

   1.   The Beginning of Egograms   3
   2.   Construction of Egograms   17
   3.   A Sampling of Egograms   35
   4.   Accuracy of Egograms   58

PART TWO: EGOGRAMS IN CHANGE AND GROWTH   79

   5.   The Elements of Change   81
   6.   Here's How—Actual Techniques
       For Personality Growth   101
   7.   The Flow of Psychological Energy,
       or The Constancy Hypothesis   122

PART THREE: EGOGRAMS IN ACTION   137

   8.   Loneliness   139
   9.   Conflicts in Coupling   154
  10.   Symptoms   184
  11.   Authority Conflicts   194

Index   205

FOREWORD

The need for this book became apparent when my students, clients, and I were confronted with the explosive psychological revolution of the last decade. Previously, many doctors with strong intellectual theories, arising mainly from the medical model, had applied logic and reason to psychological problems; unfortunately these analytic processes were laborious, time-consuming, and expensive for most people. At the same time, vigorous new programs relying upon the direct expression of feeling and emotion were developing, mainly from outside the medical community. These programs proved effective in freeing people to experience the raw passions inside themselves. Disappointingly, the effects frequently wore off quickly and sometimes the application of techniques was haphazard. The egogram, its theory and its use, is the result of the marriage of the intellectual approach on the one hand, and the emotional, "feeling" approach on the other.

"Egogram"* is a term coined to describe a simple method by which an individual can see himself/herself and others in a meaningful way that leads to creative action. Designed to be read independently from other works on Transactional Analysis, this book includes a brief introduction to basic TA ideas. Part I gives the principles of egograms and includes a sample of several important personality types. Part II is concerned with the processes which occur during psychological and social growth, the resistances encountered, and the specific action necessary to bring about desired changes. Part III uses the case histories of commonly occurring problems to illustrate how individuals have enriched their lives by their own efforts.

---

*This is a neologism of mine. Don't look for it in the dictionary—yet.

Egograms would not have been possible without the pioneering work of Dr. Eric Berne, first my teacher and later my friend and colleague, whose honest intellect and unfailing wish to provide effective treatment for his clients was unselfishly shared. Berne was the father of Transactional Analysis, and, additionally, he created a living forum whereby the childlike needs of curiosity could be met and combined with rigorous scientific thought. This was possible through the formation of the San Francisco Transactional Analysis Seminars, of which the International Transactional Analysis Association was an outgrowth.

I am indeed grateful to many of the members of the TA family who offered constructive criticism and uses for the egogram concept. Franklin Ernst, M.D., Kent Hinesley, M.D., Stephen B. Karpman, M.D., Ken Ernst, and I were the original volunteers for the first experiment in egograms. I owe special thanks to Dr. Karpman for applying his keen intellect to these newly evolving ideas as the past president of the San Francisco Transactional Analysis Seminars, editor-in-chief of the *Transactional Analysis Journal,* and a long-time friend. Likewise Claude Steiner, Ph.D., whose work on scripts was especially inspirational. Dr. Steiner—one of the original members of the seminars—contributed so much to my ideas and was, to me, like a brother in those exciting years. Barbara Miller, R.N., and George David, M.D., expended a good deal of their time and creativity to further egogram exploration and development, for which I am deeply appreciative. John Kendra, Ph.D., was the first to present independent research in comparing the egograms of people with suicidal tendencies. Many others in the TA organization have been inspirational through the work they have done in developing their own new theories which have been applicable to egograms, particularly Jacqui Schiff, M.S.S.W., and many of her associates; Robert Goulding, M.D. and Mary Goulding, M.S.W., of the Western Institute for Group and Family Therapy; Francisco Del Casale, M.D., of Buenos Aires, Argentina, with whom I spent several evenings discussing egogram ideas; Mary Boulton, Ph.D., of the Gotham Institute of Transactional Analysis in New York City;

and Jaswant Singh, Ph. D., Carlos and Saroj Welch, and Father George Kandathil, all of India.

Outside the TA movement several people have been most influential in the formation of my ideas on the egogram: Jacob Moreno, M.D., developer of psychodrama, with whom I studied briefly in New York, and especially his associates on the West Coast, Martin Haskell, Ph.D., and his wife Rochelle, who have been instrumental in presenting action techniques; Fritz Perls, M.D., the founder of Gestalt, and many of his followers whose techniques have been eye-opening; Rollo May, M.D., with whom I studied in New York and whose existential attitude seems compatible with my methods; Joseph Campbell, the mythologist, who has superbly described to me the universal occurrence of different images and forces which are complementary to this work; and innumerable people who lived and shared their humanism at Esalen on the Big Sur coast— their spirit is remembered.

My heartfelt thanks also go to the many trainees and clients who have contributed to the development of egograms. Indeed, most of the work on egograms was done in actual group settings. Their enthusiasm and inventiveness made all of these ideas possible.

Bobbi Ricca and Carole Krumland invested far more than secretarial skills; Peggy Thiel, who was originally hired as the typist, blossomed with creativity to contribute a valuable idea to the manuscript; and my good friend Bob Silverstein of Quicksilver added substantially to the development of the book, acting as a truly inspiring force. I also owe a measure of thanks to Marie Cantlon of Harper & Row for her help in organizing the flow of the text.

More than anyone else my wife Katherine, to whom this book is dedicated, has been my greatest inspiration. Many ideas have become crisp because of her efforts. As an editor of the entire manuscript, she has not only contributed an academic critique and important additions to the theory, but also given freely of her love.

—JOHN M. DUSAY, M.D.
San Francisco, 1976

IMPORTANT WORDS

Doctors have often been accused by their patients of using big words, and rightfully so. Unfortunately, this does more than just confuse issues; it tends to elevate the doctor to a lofty, mystical position while reducing the patient to feelings of being "inferior." This is little short of disastrous in the field of mental health. It takes only a few sessions in my practice for clients to learn the key vocabulary, the seven words given below. Time and energy are not wasted on trying to decode a complex jargon, but rather are spent on getting better. Because the language is simple, I feel that this book can be read as meaningfully by a farmer with a third-grade education as by a professor of symbolic logic.

The words "Parent," "Adult," and "Child," when capitalized, refer to *egostates.* These have a special, but easily learned definition, which is expressed in the colloquial language familiar to those with some knowledge of Transactional Analysis. Likewise "Game," Script," and "Stroke" have special meanings easily learned by the reader.

The use of "He" and "She" is in approximately the same proportion throughout the book. When sexual differences are important, they are stated, and from time to time I have purposefully used He/She to bring attention to the fact that by the mere use of habitual pronouns, archaic attitudes may be reinforced at the expense of one group of people or another. Although it makes it slightly more cumbersome to read, the semantic awareness which is facilitated is worth the effort to me. "Doctor-patient" has been replaced by "Therapist-client" to emphasize the equal footing of two people embarking upon a mutual endeavor.

All the examples given in this book are highly disguised and some are composites so that anonymity is completely preserved. The key transactions and principal happenings are, however, accurate and true presentations. Certain technical and philosophical issues are broadened in the section at the end of each chapter entitled Footnotes for Philosophers—an annotated bibliography for follow up by serious students.

Introduction:

Evolution of Egograms

The most important rule of human psychological growth is that a person's life is enriched as a direct result of his or her *own* efforts. While a spiritual leader may provide inspiration, a doctor may catalyze change, and a "group movement" may provide support and comradery, the ultimate power and responsibility for attaining one's potential lies squarely with each person. However, such effort alone is not enough. Energy must be exerted in the right *direction.* How each person can create a unique blueprint for change, and both develop and channel the forces of his or her personality in the right direction, is the gist of this book. A true story about a boyhood hero of mine who fulfilled his ultimate goals in life against great odds clearly demonstrates that positive change is indeed possible.

Eight-year-old Glenn Cunningham fought into the burning building to rescue his brother. The flames nearly overwhelmed him, his brother died, and his own legs were so badly burned that the doctors thought they would have to be amputated. Glenn did not passively accept his "fate" but steadfastly refused this operation. After many unsuccessful attempts, he began to walk again. He put himself on a strict physical regimen which included exercise and proper diet. He ran on the plains through the western Kansas wind whenever he could; eventually, he joined the university track team. There, in 1934, Glenn Cunningham surged through the final lap and raced into world history as the fastest man alive. His record time of 4 minutes 4 seconds for the one-mile race was held as the international standard until 1945. Most important in this example of physical triumph was the way in which Glenn committed both his time and his energy to strengthening the weak physical parts of his enfeebled body.

Years later, a man's victory over a psychological obstacle every bit as dramatic unfolded. There was scarcely a dry eye in the therapy room when fifty-year-old George Foster announced "I have won the struggle, and it's time to say goodbye to you." The setting was a group therapy session in 1975 and the listeners were old friends by now, people who had intimately shared their lives with him. For years, George had habitually drunk himself into pseudo-euphoric states, attempting to erase the painful memory of his mother who had abandoned him at the age of three. After being moved from one foster home to another, he eventually made a powerful childhood decision: "Nobody wants me." For the next thirty-five years, this decision dictated the pattern his life would take—through a broken marriage and unhappy affairs. His one solace was alcohol, and he would turn to it whenever his "real" world became too painful. His psychological state of mind, that of an angry, unwanted little boy, was as crippling to him as Glenn Cunningham's scarred legs. He dragged his feelings of rejection with him wherever he went—into work, into marriage, and eventually into the therapist's office. This part of him, the alternately hurt and angry little boy, could be seen years later in his gestures, his conversations, his vocabulary, his voice tones, and in his dejected appearance. He seldom looked at people, and would furtively glance at others in a flinching manner, as if he wore a sign saying, "Please reject me." By looking for rejection, he found it, and this reinforced his basic belief that he was not wanted.

Because this behavior pervaded his entire life, his other personality aspects were weak and underdeveloped. He seldom laughed or had fun, he avoided making decisions, and he neither stood up for his own rights nor involved himself in other people's problems. Some emotional parts of George Foster stood out clearly; others were dormant or unused. George's personality composite—his "vibrations" to others—are reflected in what is called his "egogram." The egogram is a visual symbol that represents the total personality of any human being by separating it into its various aspects and clearly showing which parts are "weak" and which are "strong."

The egogram deals with all the human passions—positive and negative—that exist in different arrangements in each of us. The egogram is like a psychological fingerprint; each person has a unique profile which can be seen and measured. In a finite sense, no two egograms are exactly the same. The egogram, by measuring the range of human psychological energy, can and will, I hope, serve as a tool for promoting positive growth.

After George and the other group members constructed each other's egogram, they gained a new awareness and fresh insight about themselves. For the first time, George was able to see how other people viewed him (which was uniform and consistent among all the members). He was also able to predict how he would relate to people in the future if he continued his pattern of using his hurt "little-boy" part. (He had a tendency to choose rejecting "friends.") Most important, George's egogram became a valuable tool that he could personally use to change and develop himself. Just as Glenn Cunningham refused to accept his scarred legs, George refused to accept the aspects of his personality that were scarred and ineffectual. Instead, he worked at strengthening and developing the positive, but initially weak, parts.

Personality components have a specific definition and can be understood by focusing on what are called *egostates,* the precursors of egograms. Eric Berne, a San Francisco psychoanalyst, made a great leap in the evolution of psychiatry when he discovered egostates, which he described in 1957 via a case presentation about a person plagued by a compulsive gambling habit. This person used a logical gambling system to increase his chances at the Nevada gaming tables. At the same time he meticulously followed his superstitious beliefs which, logically, did not help his chances. After a winning spree, he would ritually take a shower back at his hotel. While walking between casinos, he carefully avoided stepping on sidewalk cracks. He used a peculiar rationale to explain his losses. If he lost $50, he would say, "I brought $100 with me and only lost $50 . . . therefore, I'm really ahead $50." His logical versus his superstitious thinking remained only interesting until a revelation occurred later when he recounted an incident that had happened to him years before. As an eight-year-old boy vacationing at a dude ranch and wearing his cowboy suit, he helped a hired man unsaddle a horse. After they finished, the hired man said, "Thanks, cowpoke." His young assistant replied, "I'm really not a cowpoke. I'm really just a little boy." Suddenly, Berne's client turned to him and said, "That's just the way I feel now. Sometimes I feel I'm not really a lawyer; I'm just a little boy." It was evident that the client employed two types of thinking in his present life. One was the effective, logical system that he used in a successful law practice; the other was a nonrational system appropriate for a little boy. It involved his avoiding cracks, taking ritual showers, and using unusual arithmetic formulas to explain his losses.

One state worked for his business functioning and the other involved his fantasies. These Berne called "egostates," and both were conscious, deliberate, visible parts of his ego system. Berne labeled one the *Child,* and observed that this part was based upon youthful archaic judgments and was, indeed, still influencing his client's daily pursuits. The other he labeled the *Adult,* which was based upon a logical, rational, and computer-like use of data. Later, Berne recognized the *Parent* egostate as that part of the individual which deals with the morals, values, and prejudices that are derived from one's actual parental figures. Quite important is the finding that these egostates are *active determinants*—they cause behavior. This was a major breakthrough in contemporary psychiatry, for no longer were we limited to exploring only the concept of the unconscious to find out what made us tick. Instead of exploring and encouraging a discussion of past experiences as Freud did, and in some respects, as Jung's therapeutic approach dictated too, Berne began watching for the unfolding of egostates in his consulting room. Our indebtedness to the liberating effects that Freud's theory originally provided is unquestioned; thanks to Berne, we now, happily, have expanded possibilities.[1]

Figure A-1 is a diagram of the structure of personality, showing distinct *boundaries* between the different states—Parent, Adult, and Child:

Figure A-1. Three Egostates

Eric Berne, myself, and other interested professionals in San Francisco studied egostates during the years 1957 through 1962. Our approach was mostly structural, somewhat anatomical, or qualitative, as we discussed what distinguished one egostate from another. At that time, we were not as concerned with the quantity of energy flowing from each of the egostates. From our studies emerged the first phase of a system which came to be known as Transactional Analysis—or TA, as it is now commonly called. As this system has been discussed thoroughly both in books written for professionals and in several popular books, I will not go into the details here except to mention the most important features.[2]

The word "transactional" evolved when Berne explored how the different egostates of one person would dramatically transact (communicate) with the different egostates of another person. He was especially concerned about the specific transactions that left people feeling bad or exploited. Berne developed a new way of looking at social behavior when he noted that people transact on two levels simultaneously: first on an obvious, overt level; and secondly on a hidden, covert level. He labeled these series of dual transactions *games*.[3] Attention to the dynamics and types of psychological games comprised the second phase of TA, between 1962 and 1966.

A psychological game diagram (Figure A-2) symbolizes one possibility that can happen when two people (or six egostates) get together:

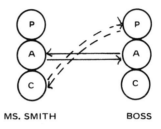

MS. SMITH   BOSS

Figure A-2. A Game Diagram

On the social level, solid arrows indicate the overt or "out-loud" message transacted; on the psychological level, the dotted arrows indicate a different, hidden message being communicated. The importance of these two-level communications is illustrated by a Ms. Smith, who gets fired from many jobs, and suffers from depression. She says to her boss on the Adult-Adult social level, "Here is your report," while on the Child-Parent psychological level, she coughs and blows smoke in his face; he, in turn, gives her a disapproving glance. She gets a hidden "payoff," a feeling of rejection, and the boss gathers one more reason to fire her. After enough games, she will be rejected—again. (This game is colloquially known as "Kick Me.")

People play games to get *strokes,* whenever more positive methods fail. When the human baby is born it must be touched in order to thrive—later the physical touching is partly replaced by verbal stroking. Playing "Kick Me" shows that negative strokes are better than no strokes at all—but TA treatment is directed toward allowing a person to get better strokes.[4]

After his discovery of egostates, transactions, and games, Berne began to focus upon the structure and details of people's *life scripts.* By analyzing scripts, one could explain why one person chooses to live his/her life in one manner while another chooses a different path. Claude Steiner constructed the first *script matrix,* which mapped out in diagrammatic form the crucial transactions in families between parents and their children.[5]

The script matrix (Figure A-3) illustrates the essential types of transactions between two parents and their developing child:

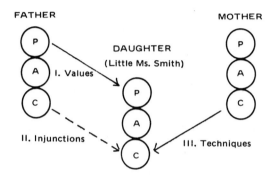

Figure A-3. A Script Matrix*

From the Parent egostate of Mother and Father come *values* (I) —such as "Please me." On a hidden level, many times nonverbally, come incompatible messages—such as "Get lost," "You are not OK,"—labeled *injunctions* (II). The same-sex parent shows how to live with the incompatible messages—such as "Smoke too much," "Take LSD"—or *techniques* (III). With this type of programming, which Ms. Smith finally accepted, it is understandable why she lived her life by "trying to please" and then getting rejected.

Berne and others studied these intimate transactions, and

*Visual symbols have had particular importance in TA. We've found it makes things simpler—a good eidetic image is worth thousands of explanatory words; even more important, symbolizing means a personal commitment— "Here's the way I see things."

made monumental contributions to the understanding of the "How I got to be myself" question.[6] This third phase of TA, *script analysis,* is still being investigated and expanded by many of Berne's followers.[7]

While TA was developing, exciting new "experiential" therapies were emerging which focused upon "feeling" and paid less attention to theory. Many people began to explore ways in which they could directly *experience* their inner pains, sadnesses, and disappointments, as well as their joys. These emotional release techniques began to gain momentum, and this appeared to indicate that people were tired of talking and were ready for active experiencing. In California during the mid-1960s and early 1970s, a cornucopia of psychological schools and therapies abounded. "Permission" groups sprang up within the TA family, and these incorporated a unique mixture of music and exercises which served to bring about heightened emotional awareness. Such groups had a notable effect upon "heavy intellectuals," who removed their neckties and shoes and began to smile. Most of this new wave, however, came from outside TA, from the evolving human potential movement. At Esalen Institute, a now famous growth center on the dramatic Big Sur coast, gurus presented diverse and innovative experiential techniques. Today, Esalen has one of the best equipped "pillow pounding" rooms I have ever seen. Other experiential influences, such as Virginia Satir's dramatic family work, Synanon (the ex-drug addict treatment program), and various body therapies which encouraged the release of anger arose, all with one primary aim in mind: to generate and deal with "feelings." The sometimes confusing array of activities ranged from nude encounter groups to serene, introspective meditation sessions. Some of the alternative psychological schools maintained a responsibility for their clients, others did not. Deleterious results were unfortunately common in the latter instances.

In my early student days with Berne, my interest was mainly in clinical research dealing with how people changed by specifically shifting the quantity of energy emanating from the various egostates. I refer to this as "egostate energy," a term which I am using to depict the strength of the utterance which is expressed from the different egostates. It is not meant to imply energy in the strict physical sense. It is likewise different from Freud's somewhat obscure discussion of the term "cathexis," which is another issue altogether, having to do with the focusing of unconscious mental energy.

I was curious about the actual processes of how people function in the "here-and-now," a phrase I first came across in Fritz Perls's *Gestalt Therapy Verbatim.* The release of feelings alone, without an effective way of dealing with these raw emotions, made little sense to me. Since TA was a practical, useful, and *complete* theory of personality, I felt it had a tremendous potential to blend with the useful "feeling" therapies—most notably, with psychodrama and Gestalt.

Berne's friends and colleagues were saddened by his death in 1970; but TA did not die with him. The weekly San Francisco seminar, a forum for generating ideas, moved to my home. These seminars without Berne became less scientific, which may have been fortunate as temporarily they took on a free-spirited, fun-loving air. After one particular session devoted to artistic expression, I can remember wiping fingerpaints off my walls and wondering what all this meant. At first these experiential activities appeared to be frivolous, but soon they gave rise to innovations and workable expansions of the original TA model.

Looking back, I can pinpoint the very occasion that prompted me to become an *"action"* therapist. I had been invited to join a panel contrasting the two developing types of popular psychotherapy: Transactional Analysis and Gestalt. Initially, I had assumed that Berne and other experienced TA people would be there, too. It was therefore jolting when I learned that the entire program was to consist of Fritz Perls, the originator of Gestalt therapy, and myself! When flair for drama, his genius for perception, and his highly competitive nature. Admittedly, Perls had a huge advantage over me—he looked just like God.*

*You'll see what I mean if you look at the photo on the jacket of his book, *Gestalt Therapy Verbatim,* Lafayette, Calif.: Real People Press, 1969.

Perls later referred to our encounter in his book, *In and Out the Garbage Pail,* by accurately commenting that he had met a young TA person who was "no match for me." Perls pulled me back and forth through an experiential "keyhole." I was well trained in TA theory and an experienced public speaker, yet I had had little experience with the strong emotional displays that are so important in life and on stage. Thinking was my strong suit. Perls was the opposite. He had a brilliant mind, but preferred to confront first and think later. At one point he discounted all parental influences, claiming that they led to an absurd "responsibility trip." Although I basically agreed with this premise, I interjected a comment that the Parent egostate was important and that many parents pass on positive values to their children. That was all Perls needed. It was as if he were waiting for this, for it set the stage for an active confrontation. He exclaimed that the Parent always pops out in time of stress. With that, he leaped up on top of the discussion table, threw back his beaded necklace, and swiftly unzipped the giant zipper on his orange jumpsuit. He nodded at the hundreds of spectators, and roared at me, "Jack, I'm going to pull out my prick!" I shouted reflexively, "Stop! Don't do it!" His eyes twinkled, his face melted into a triumphant smile, and he slid into his seat gloatingly and said, "See! I pulled out your Parent."

Perls's lively demonstration nearly finished me off. I sheepishly resumed my place behind the podium and began to muse over my reliance on rational methods. My formal scientific background and skills, like that of many medical doctors, had not lent itself to the development of a free, uninhibited, spontaneous approach. I had been questioning the relevancy of the many years I had spent in formal psychiatric training, believing that if I could convey logical explanations, my clients would get better. Perls shook this belief with his exuberant Free Child and hastened my drive to become an active therapist. For me, the fourth phase—the action stage— of TA had definitely arrived.

Essentially, Perls was right. Both the expression and the eruption of feelings are vastly important for human change.

Eric Berne was also right. The use of clear, logical thinking and intuition as it pertains to human development is equally vital. The eruption of emotion promotes growth when combined with logical analysis.[8] When both the feeling and thinking parts of a person are united, the ground for creative potential is fertile.

This book is about egograms, and hence, about people, about how we broadcast our rich and complex inner selves in the "here-and-now." We can view ourselves and others accurately, then use this potent tool to facilitate change, action, and growth.

FOOTNOTES FOR PHILOSOPHERS

1. E. Berne, *Transactional Analysis in Psychotherapy,* New York: Grove Press, 1961. Eric Berne once remarked that a theory or belief in the unconscious was not necessary for the application of Transactional Analysis (TA). He did mention the word "unconscious" in 1961 (footnote 3) when referring to life scripts as being "an unconscious life plan." This was during the early development, prior to the script matrix and the bringing-to-awareness of the injunction. In all fairness to those of the Freudian psychoanalytic persuasion, Berne never did give up his belief in a dynamic unconscious—as he mentioned dreams, parapraxis, and infantile sexuality as proof. Several of his followers, including Claude Steiner and myself, seriously questioned his position.
2. See, for instance, T. Harris, *I'm OK, You're OK,* New York: Harper & Row, 1969. This is a popular layman's guide to TA. Likewise, M. James and D. Jongeward, *Born to Win,* Reading, Mass.: Addison-Wesley, 1971.
3. E. Berne, *Games People Play,* New York: Grove Press, 1964.
4. Without sufficient touching, human infants fail to thrive: R. Spitz, "Hospitalism: Genesis of Psychiatric Conditions in Early Childhood," in *Psychoanalytic Study of the Child,* 1:53, 1945. Monkeys don't fare well either without strokes: H. Harlow, "Love in Infant Monkeys," *Scientific American,* June, 1959.
5. C. Steiner, *Scripts People Live,* New York: Grove Press, 1974.
6. E. Berne, *What Do You Say After You Say Hello?,* New York: Grove Press, 1972.

7. Confronted with these messages, the life script becomes final when the Child *decides* to accept the messages. (The amount of *responsibility* for the choice at a young age is debatable—he or she is much smaller than the actual parents.) See R. Goulding, "New Directions in Transactional Analysis: Creating an Environment for Redecision and Change," in *Progress and Family Therapy*, edited by C. Sager and H. Kaplan, New York: Bruner and Mazel, 1972. Also J. Schiff, "Reparenting," *Transactional Analysis Journal* (cited herafter as *TAJ*), vol. 1, no. 1., January 1971.

8. While Berne's system originally started with an intuitive flash from his lawyer client, he relied very heavily upon logic, and many of his followers in TA became technically proficient, causal and logical. This was very similar to Freud's technique of looking for a linear cause and effect explanation for human psychological development. Recently, Robert Ornstein, in *The Psychology of Consciousness* (W. H. Freeman and Company, San Francisco, 1972.), distinguished between the right-handed and left-handed types of thinking—the right-handed side (left hemisphere of the brain) being the logical, while the left-handed side (the right hemisphere of the brain) generates the intuitive, mystical knowing. Dr. Jose A. Arguelles, in *The Transformative Vision*, Berkeley and London: Shambhala Press, 1975, by studying art history has shown how the flow of civilization has gone between what he calls the "techne and the psyche." He analogizes the "techne" as belonging to the right-handed way—the technical, causal part which has been in ascendance in Western civilization for the past 400 years—and as a process pertaining more to the stereotyped masculine image, which is also scientific. In contrast the psyche, which is the left-handed side, is the more intuitive—the knowing without being burdened with causality, the gradual unfolding, an Oriental way—which is more expressed in the stereotyped feminine way. He sees the middle road, a combination between these, as being extremely important. He points out that in Western civilization, we have an overbalance of the logic or techne at the present time. Berne's system seems to have been more technical, while many new psychologies, particularly Gestalt, seem more perceptive, intuitive, bent on confronting rather than explaining in a causal way. A balance of both techne and psyche results from blending TA and Gestalt.

PART ONE

PRINCIPLES OF EGOGRAMS

1

The Beginning of Egograms

An egogram, simply defined, is a bar graph showing the relationship of the parts of the personality to each other and the amount of psychological energy emanating outward. It has been found that a unique profile exists for each individual. The egogram is based on intuition and is logically constructed—born of the cooperation between the "feeling" and "thinking" sides of the observer. The figure below (Figure B-1) shows the five basic functional parts of the personality:

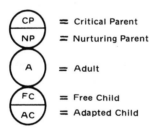

Figure B-1. Functional Egostates

The Parent has both Critical and Nurturing aspects; the Adult remains undivided; and the Child is seen with both its Free and its Adapted functions. For expediency, these are written as the Critical Parent (CP), the Nurturing Parent (NP), the Adult (A), the Free Child (FC), and the Adapted Child (AC).

The function of each of the egostates is simple: the Critical Parent is the part of the personality that criticizes or finds fault;

the Nurturing Parent nurtures and promotes growth; the Adult is for logic and precision; the Free Child is for fun and frivolity; while the Adaptive Child conforms and compromises.

None of the five functional egostates is inherently "good" or "bad," since all functions may be used either in a positive or a negative way. A transecting vertical line illustrates the presence of both negative and positive aspects in each of the five egostates and thus gives a total picture of functional personality (Figure B-2):

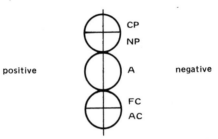

Figure B-2. Functional Egostates (Positive and negative qualities)

For example, the Critical Parent may say, "You're an ass," which implies a negative "putdown" statement. Or, the Critical Parent may say to a three-year-old girl, "I told you to get out of the street," and save her life.

While the figure above shows "what" is being considered, it does not show "how much." This is the job of the egogram.

The lower horizontal bar symbolizes the reservoir of life energy which can be channeled into the vertical columns in a fluid way. The circle shows that individual parts make up a whole (Figure B-3).

Everyone constructs primitive mental egograms without knowing it while going about their daily pursuits. Consider Wanda, who has stepped off the bus and is beginning the two-block walk to her office one morning. As she waits on the corner for the traffic light to change, she spots an unsavory character. Intuitively, she tenses up and shys quickly away from him. On the surface he looks all right, but Wanda has detected a cruel, hostile attitude and veers away from his presence.

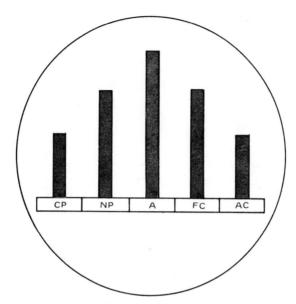

Figure B-3. An Egogram

Wanda made an instantaneous personal diagnosis, and might even be at a loss to explain exactly how she arrived at her conclusion. These types of judgments are the common everyday thought processes that everyone goes through—sorting out the good guys from the bad guys. Wanda actually formulated her opinion without witnessing this man's social behavior with another person. The total sum of Wanda's life experience culminated at that moment. Wanda knew, and accurately so, that the stranger had a preponderance of critical energies, the other forces being far lower (Figure B-4).

A little later, Wanda passed Joy, a sparkling, smiling, bubbly girl. Their eyes met, and they exchanged spontaneous smiles. Wanda thought, "Isn't she pleasant! Wouldn't she make a nice friend?" Joy's vibrations conveyed friendliness, playfulness, and a childlike openness. Wanda's archaic* diagnosis of Joy revealed a large amount of Free Child (Figure B-5).

*In this sense, archaic, means pre-logical; intuitive or knowing without knowing why.

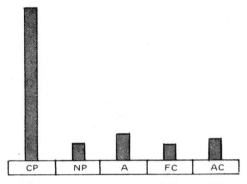

Figure B-4. Unsavory Character's Predominant Egostate

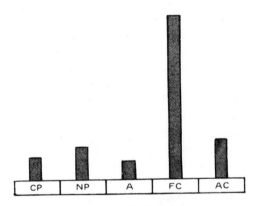

Figure B-5. Joy's Predominant Egostate

Next, as Wanda was daydreaming, she stumbled into a "scientific type." His face bore the blank expression of a digital computer, and Wanda intuited this person to be punctual, exacting, and perfectionistic. She immediately felt bored by such a cerebral man, and yawned a bit. She sensed him to be like the person described by the egogram in Figure B-6.

Wanda glanced at her watch and discovered that she had only twenty minutes to grab a quick bite before work. She sailed into the Yum Yum Cafe and plopped down on a stool.

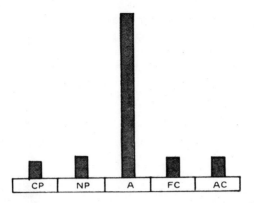

Figure B-6. Scientific Man's Predominant Egostate

Nourishing Nelly smiled from behind the counter and soothed, "What will it be, dearie?" Wanda felt relaxed, comfortable, in good hands. Nourishing Nelly would be an ideal lady to confide in, discuss her problems with, and seek advice from; and indeed, Nelly was frequently in this role while dispensing doughnuts. (Nourishing Nellie can as frequently be a social worker, nurse, psychotherapist, and/or a close friend.) Wanda enjoyed her soft, jovial, concerned attitude and wanted to hug her. Here is Nellie's predominant feature (Figure B-7):

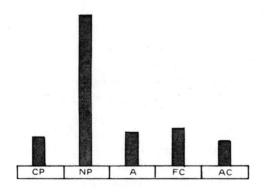

Figure B-7. Nourishing Nellie's Predominant Egostate

At the end of the counter, Wanda spotted a Loser. She was aware of this even before he began talking to his friend about losing his job, his money, and his wife. Wanda's instantaneous impression looked like this (Figure B-8):

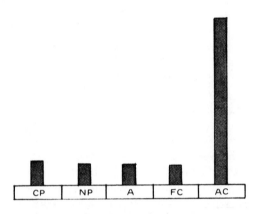

Figure B-8. The Loser's Predominant Egostate

Wanda would quickly respond to her initial first impressions of others. She was always accurate on another person's highest egostate, and these archaic impressions governed her actions toward them.

People are able to differentiate between a loving and a hostile potential in a person. Heroes and villains, losers and winners, exist in all cultures in varying degrees. Wanda's morning stroll to work is characteristic of what happens to every person every day; it serves to explain why some people duck away behind their newspapers from certain types of people and go out of their way considerably to be in the presence of others. These maneuvers are not accidental; they are based upon the responses to the instantaneous diagnosis of others' basic parts. These intuitive perceptions become habitual from early life and it seems that they are unconscious, while a more apt explanation is that they are so routine that there is no *focus* upon their day-to-day functions. The colloquial term "vibrations," popularized during the 1960's, seems to have been well chosen to describe these perceptions of the way another person is "coming on." The following case of Mary shows how these simple vibrations unite to form what is called an egogram.

MARY'S ORGASM

Mary's case is historical in that she had the first egogram which was formally devised. Her story serves to illustrate the general characteristics of all egograms.

Mary was a beautiful twenty-six-year-old pre-orgasmic woman,* who turned to me as a psychiatrist to work on her "sexual hang-up."[1] After consultation with her gynecologist, it was ascertained that her condition was psychological rather than physical, as is usually the case. We agreed to work for her goal of attaining sexual satisfaction and achieving orgasm. I invited her to attend an ongoing TA group of seven people, who met for two hours once a week to analyze and improve their personal relations.[2] Mary impressed us as being well educated, worldly, and sexually liberated. She had experienced sexual relations with various men, including a long-term, loving relationship as well as a "one-night stand"; she felt neither guilty about sex nor sexually fulfilled.

When asked if any of her girlfriends were experiencing problems similar to hers, she replied, "I wouldn't know. I don't talk to people about *their* problems." This statement later became the giveaway clue about her personality structure. She was employed at a challenging, scientific job which gave her deep satisfaction. She was not opposed to marriage or having a family, but was not in a hurry for either. Mary was also creative and artistic, and performed modern dance with a local group.

In psychotherapy, she worked hard in her group at analyzing her problems.** She remained receptive to the suggestions about enhancing enjoyment, and would eagerly use her fine

---

* "Pre-orgasmic" is an accurate, benevolent term. "Nonorgasmic" sounds fateful; and "frigid" is more appropriate for refrigerators than people.

** The group of seven people had various treatment goals. They met once a week for two hours and concentrated their energies on each person attaining his or her treatment contract. TA was the primary method utilized.

sense of humor when telling sexual jokes. Mary had read the popular sex manuals and experimented with their remedies: oils, lotions, massage, and different positions. She considered herself to be an OK person, and it surprised everyone that with all of her positive qualities and hard work, there was no resolution of her complaint.

In her TA group, Mary learned to identify her own egostates, and became aware of which ones she was in. She found her favorite game to be "Do Me Something," whereby she would entice others to help her out, and then switch and make sure that they couldn't. Her little-girl smile would constantly frustrate their efforts. "Do Me Something" is a common sexual game, which emerged as a repetitive pattern of hers. When her partner asked, "Did you have one?" she would reply sweetly, "Almost, but not quite." (What happens in a psychotherapy group also happens outside the group.) Her therapy group caught onto her pattern and took an antithetical stance. They encouraged her to be independent and solve her own problems. They did not "bite" on her pleas for rescues.

Mary began having difficulty in structuring her time because she was unable to get others to play her usual game and "help" her. When a group member suggested that as an alternative, she could help other people, she responded, "Fine, I'll *analyze* their difficulties." With her strong scientific and analytical mind, she proceeded to make brilliant interpretations about other group members' problems. Mary's energies became concentrated in her Adult egostate, yet lacked a caring, nurturing quality. This activity curtailed her game of "Do Me Something," and was refreshing to Mary, but she still did not realize sexual satisfaction.

She reminisced about how her parents influenced her early upbringing. A complete script analysis was done on her life, and her predominant values turned out to be: "Work hard and be successful." Her parents had both worked full time and exercised the work ethic; unfortunately, they didn't seem to have much interest in their children, despite the fact that the mechanics of the household were run well. The parents emphasized "independence," "success," and "intelligence" to her, but as they were both busy, they had little time or energy left over for nurturing Mary. Because of this, she neither learned how to accept nurturing nor how to give it. Being sensitive, her parents realized that they were falling short and felt somewhat guilty about their busy schedules and lack of home life, which Mary decided to exploit. This explains how she developed the game of "Do Me Something" early in life as an attempt to get some parenting from her otherwise easy-to-live-with parents. Play was also notably lacking in her early days.

Mary at first thought that contacting her deepest feelings—crying, shouting, and expressing joy—would help her bring about sexual release. She tried many things: massage classes (for bodily awareness), encounter groups (to uncover deep feelings), and undertook a stint at psychodrama, art therapy, and various other weekend growth groups. Colloquially known as the California Group Growth Scene, these were some of the various new therapies which were being tried out at the time. She enjoyed such endeavors and found some to be invaluable as growth and learning experiences. Still, she did not attain orgasm. (Realizing that weekend encounter groups alone are not sufficient for orgasm, it should be noted that she did meet several exciting young men there.)

Almost ready to give up, we scheduled a private review session and Mary asked, "What's missing?" The night before, I had fallen asleep while reading an article that contained bar graphs, and being perplexed about why she had not been successful, said, "I'm not sure, but let's do an experiment." A bar graph was drawn on the blackboard, and the five personality components were labeled underneath. Mary and I then began to construct a diagram expressing the relative intensity of her five egostates. Mary's curiosity was "hooked," and she noted that her Adult was pretty high, and indicated that this was so. Her Free Child didn't seem to be nearly as high as her Adult, because she acknowledged spending more time analyzing why she didn't enjoy sex and reading intelligent books about it than she did having climaxes. Her Critical Parent was seen as relatively high, so a lot was put in that column. Her "feel bads" about not being fulfilled, and her game playing—as well as all the running around trying to find solutions—were part of her Adapted Child "trying" hard. This was the highest. At that point, Mary looked at the blackboard with a sudden inspiration. "Well, I guess that's it." We exchanged knowing glances, then Mary said, "I can see what my problem is. There's no Nurturing Parent—well, give me a smidgen anyway."* In her very first interview, she had given this clue, by saying that she didn't know anything about her friends' problems—with a low Nurturing Parent, she simply was not interested. This is what her egogram looked like at that moment (Figure B-9):

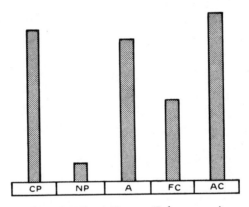

Figure B-9. Mary's Egogram (Before orgasm)

This bar graph was later labeled the *egogram* and was introduced into the group; the members immediately became excited with their new tool. They put their heads together for a solution to Mary's situation. Each member also quickly drew a personal impression of Mary's egogram and they were not surprised when they unanimously agreed that Mary's Nurturing Parent was seldom used. The deficiency now stood out like a red flag. Many suggestions were raised as to how she might raise her Nurturing Parent; one woman who was abundantly nurturing toward others, colloquially known as Big Mama, rec-

*I have never seen anyone who had a complete absence of any egostate.

ommended that she try cooking for others.* Mary laughed and discarded this idea by saying, "That's absurd. I don't even know how to boil water!" But because she had never cooked before (her boyfriends got salami and beer at her apartment), she hesitantly decided that it would certainly be a novel experience. So she announced rather dramatically that she was going to join a local cooking school.

At the next group meeting, Mary said that she had absentmindedly forgotten her earlier decision to attend a cooking school and that she would get on with it. This was a strong commitment to external action (external to the "here-and-now" of the group), rather like a prescription to be taken outside the doctor's office. The following week, when asked about it, she looked annoyed and said, "I signed up, but couldn't find the damned place."[3] The group reminded her of her high IQ, and the excellent probabilities of her being able to find a well-advertised address in the city. At this, Mary had a temper tantrum, and made a furious exit from the group session by loudly slamming the door. The next week, she returned and said somewhat sheepishly, "I guess this is known as resistance." I replied, "Yes," and at the following meeting Big Mama said reassuringly, "Don't worry, it'll feel better after you get into it." Mary finally began attending cooking classes, but would complain bitterly about them. Many group members did congratulate her for being persistent. After a number of weeks, she began mentioning some of the special recipes she was learning. Her excitement and enthusiasm mounted until she gradually developed into a gourmet cook. She enrolled in more classes and discussed the personal thrills she had when cooking for others. It was noted that her enthusiasm for culinary excellence soon rivaled her quest for orgasms. Shortly after that, at midnight, she called me excitedly on the telephone and exclaimed, "It happened! Under the table, right after the Peach Melba!" At the next group meeting Mary had a gleam in her eye, and everybody knew what had happened. The group constructed her post-orgasm egogram (Figure B-10):

*See "Big Mama" Chapter Nine, for the problem of too much nurturing.

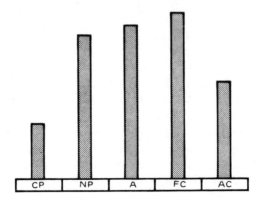

Figure B-10. Mary's Egogram (After orgasm)

This egogram depicts a profound change in Mary's personality. The energy which had previously been expended in her Critical Parent had shifted into her Nurturing Parent and some of her Adapted Child had switched into her Free Child. This was readily apparent to the other members. Mary even brought homemade cookies and passed them around in a nonchalant way. This spontaneous nurturing was an observable phenomenon of her being different. Mary felt comfortable with this newly discovered aspect of herself and freely nurtured despondent group members by saying things like, "Let's work on your problems; you look so unhappy." This was in marked contrast to her initially sitting back and looking at the clock to make sure she was getting the allotted amount of time for herself. Mary was able to sympathize, nurture, and show care for others, and simultaneously, to have more fun and satisfaction for herself. She remembered a message that her father had given her, but failed to follow himself: "You have to give, to get." When she related this precept to her orgasms, she said chuckling, "That's just tit for tat."

Mary's "pre-cure" and "post-cure" egograms represent that shift of energy coming from the various egostates.[4] Mary's egogram became the visual tool which enabled her to identify her deficits; it also pointed out clearly the specific changes she would need to undergo in order to achieve her goal. Her initial discomfort was well worth it, because of the long-term, successful results.*

FOOTNOTES FOR PHILOSOPHERS

1. Seventy years ago, Freud presented cases of conversion hysteria where women with this "affliction" would develop bodily disorders, paralysis, spasms, etc., and complained that they had either thought of or experienced sex—See the case of Dora, *Fragment of an Analysis of a Case of Hysteria* from J. Stachey, (ed.), *The Standard Edition of the Complete Psychological Works of Sigmund Freud*, Vol. VII (1901–1905), London: The Hogarth Press, 1953. Today, the norm has become the opposite—clients now say that sex isn't good enough, frequent enough, or intense enough. The pendulum of openly seeking sexual gratification seems to have swung in the opposite direction. To have made sex respectable is one of the most influential "fallouts" of Freud's genius.
2. Dr. W. Masters, addressing the 128th Annual Meeting of the American Psychiatric Association at Anaheim, California, in May 1975, reiterated that in all his experience of treating sexual dysfunction, he never treated male impotence or female nonorgasm problems per se; rather, his methods focused on personal relationships (as well as education). A major reason is the tendency of people to view themselves critically and place undo emphasis on performance—what he and his associates call "spectator/performance" problems. In reading this case history, the wisdom of that approach becomes clear—and further advances in "relationship" work will be apparent.
3. Mary was playing "Stupid," a game popular with intelligent people who wish to remain in a little-girl or little-boy position. Freudian techniques would involve psychoanalyzing the resistances, while TA techniques would aim at confronting and interrupting the destructive behavior (the concept of resistance is discussed at length in Chapter Six). This leaves the person in a temporarily disturbed but more creative, decision-making position. Because

---

*The first time an out-of-shape, flabby person decides to jog, it is a tremendous struggle. Later, after persisting and overcoming one's resistance, jogging becomes quite easy and natural.

the individual may be vulnerable and needy at this point, the transactional analyst is there to provide the permission, protection, and potency. (The first two of this trio were discussed by P. Crossman in "Permission and Protection," *Transactional Analysis Bulletin* [cited hereafter as *TAB*], vol. 5, no. 19, 1966, 152–153).

4. It is important to emphasize that expressing more nurturing is not beneficial for everyone, only for persons of either sex who have a a very low NP. I recommend cooking classes and other nurturing activities as frequently for men as for women. Chapter Seven explores the theory of shifting energy.

2

Construction of Egograms

We have drawn thousands of egograms in my TA groups over the past five years. If you wish to draw your own, or someone else's, follow these proposed simple steps—which are the same instructions for constructing egograms that I give in my groups.

1. Draw a horizontal line on a piece of paper. Underneath this, label from left to right in five equal spaces, CP (Critical Parent); NP (Nurturing Parent); A (Adult); FC (Free Child); and AC (Adapted Child).

CP	NP	A	FC	AC

Example

2. Think of a likely candidate. (It's a little tricky to draw your own; try the first one on an acquaintance.)
3. Draw whatever you "sense" or "feel" is the most predominant part of that person, and draw it in with a vertical column. (This will be the highest column.)
4. Next, draw your hunch of the lowest part of the personality as it is in comparison to the others. (This will be the lowest column.)
5. Fill in the other lines—don't worry about the exact heights of the columns because this is a relationship diagram.

17

The first hunch is generally the correct one, since intuition is the indispensable ally. Regardless of where the person is seen or how long you've known him/her, the same egogram will probably result. At a dinner party, a funeral, or on a mountain-climbing expedition, and irrespective of the time spent together—moments, months, or years—it would come out about the same. By following these simple instructions in an intuitive state, the egogram drawer will be correct around 80 percent of the time; the rest of this section is designed for improving on the 20 percent that one may miss.

Occasionally, people attempting to construct egograms start with ruled paper and percentage marks. This Adult approach looks scientific; however, laboring over percentages may ruin the intuitive forces necessary to draw a meaningful portrait and is best avoided.

By learning to recognize the specific clues and signs of different egostates, a solid body of knowledge is built up from which the intuition can flow. For instance, a surgeon may spend years learning the anatomical structures of the body and the different uses of her surgical equipment.[*] When performing an operation, she does not laboriously ponder these considerations; instead, she works freely, effortlessly, and the work flows like a symphony. If an unexpected crisis arises, she may review the fundamentals that are specifically applicable to her task. Because of her secure background, she is free to react quickly and effectively.

CLUES AND SIGNS OF EGOSTATES

In viewing the complexities and perplexities of human beings, the fundamental factors which play upon the five senses are the principal elements incorporated into the egogram. The total finished picture resembles a completed mosaic rather than dissected, individual elements. Without first mastering the fundamentals, the viewer may be overwhelmed (like the ship's cook called upon to perform an appendectomy).

[*]There are more than 2500 women surgeons in the United States at present.

Here I should distinguish between what is known as "head-tripping" and using the "intellect." The person who needlessly goes over logical details is head-tripping. When a thoughtful review is really needed, on the other hand, the person responds by thinking.

The Five Standard Senses

HEARING

Listening for specific words and tip-off sentences will yield important data. Persons who say "should," "must," "for your own good," and so on, are operating from their Parent egostate. It is not unusual for a person to incorporate the exact expression, tone, and inflection that his real, biological parents once used. The phrases, "What am I supposed to do here?" and "Do you think it would be good for me?" are spoken in a higher voice; they imply a "helpless" little boy or girl wanting very hard to please, which is indicative of the Adapted Child.

Phrases such as "The probabilities are . . .", "It seems as if . . .", or "I think . . ." are characteristic of the logical Adult egostate. Vocabulary coming from the exuberant, spontaneous Free Child, is obvious and frequently consists of only one syllable: "WOW!" Nurturing Parent statements may include such phrases as: "You seem tired today," or "May I help you?" Each person has special, unique word patterns which give clues to his or her underlying psychological behavior.

For example, Dabney walked nervously into his first group psychotherapy session, sat down, exchanged a few social pleasantries, and then, with a pleading look at me, said, "What are we supposed to do here?"[1] He persisted in a rapid-fire sequence: "Are we supposed to talk to each other? Or do you ask the questions?" Hoping he would make a declarative statement, I interrupted the bombardment by responding, "State what you are coming here for." Dabney replied, "Well, I'm supposed to take better care of myself, I should help with the chores around the house, and I'm told that I should get a job." Dabney's use of "supposed to" and "should" was noticeable and prevalent in his first session.* A tape recorder was employed in the group so that people could hear how they sounded to others and it was occasionally played back. Upon reviewing a group of tapes one evening, I began a tally sheet on the frequency of Dabney's "should" and "supposed to." He consistently used these words ten times more than anyone else in each two hour session. This curious discovery about his childlike questions distinguished Dabney from the others in a specific, quantifiable manner. (This was the initial clue leading to my experiment with shifting psychological energy.)

Dabney's stated reason for being in psychotherapy was that he "should be" more independent. In actuality, he was a well-read, bright individual with a college education. But those attributes were overwhelmed by his response to a smothering mother who thrived upon his dependence on her. In spite of the situation, part of Dabney yearned for independence, and he exhibited this desire to me by saying, "I would like to make at least $60 a week in take-home pay." This wasn't much but it represented the necessary amount of money that Dabney needed to achieve independent living away from his mother. The group agreed that his goal was valid, and this mutual agreement, called a treatment contract, was then formalized. Dabney's current job paid only $1 per hour. Because he was underpaid, his employer put up with his eccentric habits and rarely criticized him for his erratic work hours. Some weeks, Dabney would work only two or three hours and hence made only $2 or $3. Other weeks, he worked ten or twelve hours. Finally—after a laborious and challenging group experience—Dabney fulfilled his treatment contract to his and the group's satisfaction, and made his $60 a week on a steady basis.

A treatment contract is an important aspect of my work—along with most T.A. therapists.[2] This is the specific, succinctly stated goal that both client and therapist agree to. It clearly implies that they are mutual allies and not struggling enemies working toward different ends.

*The first few utterances in a group are often the most important, standard, reliable phrases that a person uses because they are pulled forth in time of stress.

Earlier, Dabney had up and down swings in both his pay-
check and his moods, which were directly contingent upon
how much work he had done that week. Studying the group
tapes, I found that there was a definite correlation between the
frequency of Dabney's "should" and "supposed to" and the
amount of money he made that week. During the weeks that he
made more money, he used these phrases far less often in the
group (see chart):

WEEK	KEY WORDS	$ EARNED
1	20	25.00
2	31	15.00
3	10	55.00
4	3	71.00
5	19	20.00

As the chart shows, there was an inverse relationship between
the use of these key words and the amount of money he made.
The following inverse relationship formula emerged:

**INCREASED PAYROLL = DECREASED "SHOULD" AND
"SUPPOSED TO"**

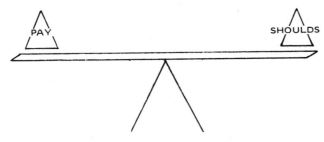

As Dabney's Adapted Child expressions decreased, he fulfilled his treatment contract. (Eventually, his usage of
"should" and "supposed to" dropped to the group norm.) His

new vocabulary included new phrases such as: "I have decided . . ." and "I think . . ." which indicated that he was shifting energy into his Adult egostate. More independence from his mother was gained by Dabney; for myself, I found that personality swings can be definitely measured, sometimes by the frequency of obvious verbal cliches, such as, "You know," or "Yes, but..."

VISION

By actually studying a person's mannerisms, gestures, bodily attitudes, walk, expressions, and postures, it is possible to form many potential judgments. This observation of "body language" and "nonverbal communication" aids in a viewer's egostate assessment and becomes a valuable perception in constructing egograms. A reprimanding, critical index finger, a raised eyebrow, and a stiff chin are certain signs of a Critical Parent. A quivering lip and an averted gaze may tip-off the viewer that the person is nervous and exhibiting a scared Adapted Child egostate. A direct, level gaze may be attributed to the Adult.[3] Subtle nuances, as well as overt gestures, are attributed to various egostates. Many people become surprised when they are confronted with their definite, giveaway mannerisms. This is known as the "25-cent photo machine" effect. When a person spends 25 cents in one of the little photographic machines, the unretouched pictures show exactly the way he/she is. Quite frequently, the person will say, "What a horrible picture," and will prefer to buy a $25 photograph which is posed and touched up.

Sometimes the words and visual clues are at odds with one another, as in giving compliments while one's fists are clenched. Mixed clues are quite important to note and frequently easy to spot. They are commonly observed, for example, in the genital game entitled "Rapo." A typical scene unfolds when a voluptuous woman sits in a cocktail lounge and positions her legs to their best advantage, exposing just enough thigh to attract the attention of a "hungry wolf." Although such scenes are common in normal boy-meets-girl situations, there is something unusual in this case. The woman's eyes convey a certain haughtiness and her rigid jaw confirms that there are two separate messages being transmitted. Her gaze is usually aimed downward at the viewer in a condescending way, but the bait is clearly her exposed thighs. Several intuitive gentlemen have picked up on her contradictory behavior and skipped by her in favor of more pleasant women. But sure enough, an intoxicated man "naively" saunters over, stares at her skirt which is gradually creeping higher and higher, and finally bites. He slurs, "Hi, sweetie! Let's me and you leave this place and have some fun." But, whammo!, our hero's jaw is slapped, and the now prim little lady hisses, "What makes you think I'm that kind of girl?" The wounded man slowly backs off, nursing his usual rejection and mumbling, "Why does this *always* happen to me?" The triumphant woman proves to herself for perhaps the thousandth time that all men are beasts, after one thing only. She consoles herself with the fact that she is able to maintain her dignity in a savage world. Important to this discussion is that all the clues were visually presented and that by recognizing them, one could easily predict the consequences. The sexually naive little-girl part along with the indignant Critical Parent resemble the fishing line which is baited and waiting for a nibble. Only those "desiring" the whammo will bite.

Impatient foot tapping, swinging legs, or drumming fingers are characteristic of the Child, as are squirming, itching, and gyrations (later replays of the mannerisms expressed when these people were little boys or little girls having to sit still in school or church). An "uptight" look, with the lips pursed tight, gives the observer the impression that he is gazing at a puckered sphincter. It appears that the jaw, the lips, and the tight facial muscles are all being pulled by an imaginary cord attached to the anus. Little kids who hold things back are quite stiff, stubborn, and relatively immobile. This "holding back" may show up at a dinner party twenty years later, where the same people look like little kids who have strayed too far from the potty.[4]

TOUCH

The original transaction is a physical action: the wiggly little sperm pushes its way into the waiting receptive egg. During the next nine months, in the protective atmosphere of the womb, an intense physical contact between the growing embryo and the mother develops. When the newborn finally squeezes its way out, the infant is met with a resounding slap on the bottom,[5] and its response is a strong outburst of crying and muscular activity. If fortunate, it finds a warm, responsive, accepting nipple. The infant's early cooing and enjoyment of being cuddled reflects the early development of trust. But if the infant enters a disturbed household, it may get a tense, cold nipple or none at all. (Harry Stack Sullivan, noted psychiatrist, once quipped that "People should choose their parents better.")

By early childhood, the various modes of physical touching and its responses are well ingrained and patterned. A little girl who is giggling in the church pew needs only to receive a firm grasp from her father and a slight shake. She will immediately respond with guilt, silence, and rapid conformity in compliance with her earlier messages. She learns two things: If she wants to be critical (Critical Parent), she should grasp tightly and shake the object of her wrath, probably her own child years later; and if she wants to express guilt (Adapted Child), she should hang her head low and tense her back muscles. Often, there are specific sensitive areas of the body unique to each individual and his/her original family, which show peculiarities and distortions. A guilt-provoking family may specialize in shaming its children and thereby induce them to hang their heads low. These people ususally suffer from upper back and neck pain, and spasms arise whenever they encounter stressful situations later in life. The hurry-up-and-do-something families produce hypertensive individuals, with tight voluntary muscles, warm red skin, and of course, rising blood pressure. The clammy, nervous, and sweaty handshake belies a frightened little child, whose parents doled out insecurities.[*]

_____

[*] Lie detector tests are partially based on these types of findings.

This is so impressive that theories of psychotherapy have been based upon the transforming of early personality development into bodily tensions.[6]

Consider the hugging exercises in an encounter group: Ed gives Beverly a hearty hug, while she awkwardly arches away from the navel down. This guarantees that no contact can occur anywhere in the genital area. Years ago, Bev's family shied away from physical touching and sexual topics were not discussed.

Hugging exercises may also demonstrate how people can feel either rejected or overwhelmed. John and Marcia hugged for several minutes, then John felt quite uneasy. During childhood, his mother only permitted hugging for a few seconds, followed by a quick release. Marcia came from a family which specialized in clinging. As a little girl, Marcia would nervously hang on to her mother, who used the threat of abandonment to keep the kids in line. Years later, Marcia held on to John tightly in an attempt to keep the huddle. The tighter she held, the more he struggled, and their touching pattern set up a feeling of being trapped for John and a feeling of rejection for Marcia. These dramatic responses can occur in just a few seconds, whether it be with a handshake or a hug.

Some people gravitate toward an actual physical touching situation. This occurred with Wanda on her way to work when she "leaned away" from the critical person and "leaned toward" Nurturing Nellie. These pre-touching avoidance and acceptance postures are readily observable and also important.

Ritualistic handshaking and touching ceremonies have been important considerations of protocol throughout civilization. Most likely, they originated as a test for discerning between friend and foe. Some classical psychoanalysts feel that it is desirable for the analyst to remain *anonymous,* and therefore insist on not shaking hands with their patients.

SMELL

This sense has been subject to ridicule and debasement in the "civilized" world. People have been taught to ignore smells. Many industries have made their fortunes with products which are designed to eradicate every possible bodily smell, their slogans claiming to make people "as fresh at the end of the day as they are at the beginning." When these smells are successfully masked, an important avenue of intuitive diagnosis is suppressed.

Prissy told about a "weird" man she had just met at a social gathering. He was a famous, successful businessman, but Prissy continually wrinkled her nose as she discussed him. When queried, she giggled with embarrassment and said, "I'm still trying to sniff him out," confessing that he didn't smell quite right to her. In a few short weeks, Prissy and the businessman stopped seeing each other, as could have been predicted by her nasal gyrations. Although few people discuss smells, relationships usually begin and terminate with the olfactory experience. Smells may even be the sensations that determine long-term affairs.[7]

Rigid nose-wrinkling decreases the size of the nasal orifice and helps prevent bad odors from entering—if it occurs in the presence of an acquaintance, there is a lousy chance for the relationship to succeed. Relaxed, naturally elongated nasal passages connote that all is well. Presumably, a perked-up nose aids a person in smelling others better.

We humans long ago gave up our reliance on our noses. Anthropologists have found evidence that early man, 30,000 years ago, accepted and later trained wild jackals, which were the ancestors of house pets. They had superior olfactory senses which aided in the survival of men, who couldn't smell dangerous approaching predators. The early men increased their chances for survival by "borrowing" the noses of dogs; the dogs, in turn, were rewarded with the logical hunting and defense tactics of man. Konrad Lorenz has theorized that the marriage of man and dog thus increased the survival of both. So *Homo sapiens* evolved away from smell long ago.[8]

Dogs and similar animal types have a very small forebrain, that part of the brain which is highly developed in humans, and enables logic, foresight, and insight to exist. But dogs do have a brain part which is relatively pronounced and highly developed, known as the rinencephalon, the old archaic part of the brain found in lower forms of animal life. It appears in animals who mainly transact by smelling. Although overshadowed by the forebrain, human beings also have a large rinencephalon, and a network of nerves which lead directly from the nose to this area. Here these nerves disperse and loop out to other areas, which include well-landmarked places that are important channels for the emotions.[9] Along this nasal-connected loop in the human brain are the centers for rage, ecstasy, hunger, fear, sexual appetite, arousal, excitement, and other emotions. Interestingly, it is very near a most unusual center which gives inordinate amounts of pleasure. When experimenters placed electrodes into this pleasure area of monkeys and then attached it to a retractable lever, the monkeys would desperately push it until they collapsed from sheer exhaustion and delight.

Certain insects emit external hormone-like substances called pheromones, which can be chemically isolated. These have been found to determine important "social" behavior. When a female moth emits this pheromone, the males from a wide radius fly furiously and undauntedly toward her, knowing just what to do. The extent to which the higher forms of life, including human beings, emit these types of smell hormones is presently unknown. It has recently been reported that certain fatty acids occur in the healthy female vagina. These chemicals vary during the monthly cycle and are most predominant during the ovulatory period, so that by the magic of nature, women may be most sexually attractive just at the moment that they are most fertile. These odiferous chemicals are the same ones that have been found to have sexually attracting properties in Rhesus monkeys. One may guess that they play an important, but hidden, role in our social judgments and hunches.[10]

TASTE

Licking and tasting other people's bodies is another taboo for human beings. Many states carry laws against "improper" tasting, with prison sentences doled out for tasting disobedience. Being a delicious part of life, it secretly happens under "acceptable" circumstances during private lovemaking. Again, animals aren't "civilized" enough to follow these prohibitions. After following their noses, they generously taste and lick one another on every available occasion. Nothing is sacred or left unlicked to their tongues—other dogs, humans, grass, leaves, and especially themselves. When dogs become sexually aroused, they gnash their teeth, salivate, and compulsively lick and chew things around the house. Human taste buds follow the commercials' directives by becoming masked with breath mints, mouthwashes, chewing gums, and sprays. A kiss becomes a packaged flavor exchange, while an ear nibble is a lovely hors d'oeuvre. Suckling mother's breast gives a very authentic bodily taste sensation; however, after the first year of life, human beings are relegated to very little of this.[11] Only after marriage is tasting acceptable—and even then it may be illegal, depending on where one lives.

While the five senses are crucial in recognizing egostate function, we have other clues and indications of which egostate is especially strong. Consider the social response as it develops in early life and recurs in later years.

Social Response

Mother demands that her four-year-old son eat his spinach, and he answers defiantly, "No—ugh—I *won't!*" This is a straightforward struggle, which may be started as the son enters the kitchen while Mother is preparing dinner (as seen in Figure C-1) and is symbolized by solid lines showing the overt message. On the other hand, when the little boy subtly turns up his nose at liver and onions, his action evokes a parental response: "You must try one bite. Don't say you don't like it before you try it." This is less straightforward and more covert, as the struggle was initiated by the little boy who wrinkled up his nose. This is "hooking," which means sending out a ploy which will snag a corresponding response from the other person. "Hooking" applies to the process taking place on a hidden level, and is involved with subtle nuances.

For instance, a husband and his wife are discussing their vacation plans—whether to go to the mountains (his choice) or the seashore (her preference). When he discusses the advantages of the mountains, she turns up her nose slightly. At this, he becomes angry and blasts her, "Go to the seashore by yourself!" In this case, the wife's turned-up nose "hooked" his parental parts and made him impervious to continuing a reasonable discussion about the merits of each resort (see Figure C-1):

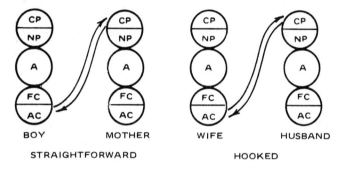

BOY   MOTHER   WIFE   HUSBAND

STRAIGHTFORWARD   HOOKED

Figure C-1.

This type of "hook" may occur at various levels: a smiling playful attitude tends to elicit pleasant smiles and winks; grumps hook grouches; persecutors hook victims; mommies hook little boys; and so on. This knowledge helps one in making a personal diagnosis. If someone frequently evokes angry, parental looks, it is reasonable to assume that he/she is "hooking" these responses by using his/her own defiant Adapted Child egostate. When a person feels like rebelling against another person, it is probably because the other is "coming on" in a pushy, parental way—much like one's own mother saying, "Eat that."

Being aware of one's own feelings and egostates when transacting with others gives an invaluable insight into one's personality.* When someone "smells a rat," there is good cause for distrust. When a man says a woman is a "turn on," it means

---

*This is a major advantage that group psychotherapy has over individual psychotherapy—there are more transactional possibilities.

he has a sexy feeling in the presence of this lady. He may astutely look for clues to ensure that the woman feels sexual "vibes" toward him. All of these situations were spawned on subtle innuendoes, and missing these clues could lead to boredom. (It is likewise important to read hostile, rejecting vibrations correctly.) Some people "flow" through life. They are adept at instantly recognizing how they affect others, and they readily know how others impress them. This does not imply that things will always go smoothly for them, but at least they will know who their friends and enemies are—*regardless of what words are spoken on the surface.*

History

Although history-taking to uncover pertinent details (which resembles listening to the words but missing the music) has been exhaustingly overworked during the last few decades, there are still instances when it is in order. For example, Archer was an accomplished index finger pointer. His finger would attack reflexively when someone else was being silly or "irresponsible." Because this was a habitual, unthinking occurrence, it went unrecognized by Archer until he was confronted with it in my therapy group. At that moment, he looked down at his still semi-erect finger and recalled vividly: "I was six years old when I accidentally spilled a huge drum of oil that my father had bought for his car all over his garage floor. He was furious when he saw the oil, and his finger came up just like my finger now. This finger is the same one that my father uses when he's angry or picking on me." It is exciting when an exact moment of fixation is remembered in its dramatic setting. Archer recalled that the oil incident happened in the summer of 1945, the year the war was over. He remembered being concerned that his angry father wouldn't let him go to the fireworks display the next day, the Fourth of July. The scolding happened at approximately 5:30 P.M., right after his father came home from work. Such poignant historical moments frequently give insights as to where, when, and how certain personality traits originated. Similarly, an astute acquaintance of mine has a particular knack for telling whether someone had an early or late, traumatic or uneventful toilet training by observing their grunts and groans in present-day activities. This may sound silly at first, but it has proven correct many times; for those readers who have never experienced these intuitive moments, attention to raising their Free Child egostate (Chapter Five) is recommended.

Re-Experiencing*

"Re-experiencing" includes historical recollections, but it proceeds further in a more lively and dramatic way. A man in a therapy group complained that he hated his nagging wife telling him to "Hurry up! Hurry up!" He recalled that his mother would rush him when he was growing up. He was told to imagine that his own mother was sitting in the empty chair which the therapist placed across from him. His visual images of his mother began to develop and when he was instructed to sit in the empty "mother's" chair, he actually became his mother. He yelled in a high voice to the seat he had just vacated, "Hurry up! Quickly! Don't you know we've got to go?" His resounding volume and sharp inflection sounded very much like the actual mother. He was told to switch back to his original seat and respond to his mother's outburst. He began to tremble and sweat; then he burst into a rage, shouting, "No! I don't want to go. I won't go! I hate you! Hate! Hate!!" He was, for those few moments, re-experiencing, or *being* the same little boy he was at age five. It was later revealed that his mother was insisting that he hurry up and go with her to her boyfriend's house. (He was jealous of his new rival.)

In group experience I have observed that about three-quarters of the people undergoing their "role playing" at first act "as if" they were pretending, much like rehearsing a role in a play. But *within only a few transactions and switches from*

*The process of re-experiencing is technically known as *surfacing*. It is described in more detail in Chapter Five.

chair to chair, the severe raw emotions emerge. This is possible in a protective and permissive setting where people don't have to hide their feelings. Everyone present who has even a little sensitivity can "feel" the switch from role play to the actual "feeling" or original experience.

An actual re-experience lays bare one's egostates while the past is relived in its most vivid form. Even if many years have passed since an impressionable experience, one's life is controlled and determined by these early events. An occasional stimulus may trigger a "lost" area and cause a person to re-experience a forgotten situation on the spot. This explains outbursts, sudden tears, and unexpected reactions. When someone is touchy or edgy, it means that his/her past experiences have taken control. In the man's case, his wife was misidentified with his mother, and she was the recipient of undeserved wrath.[12]

These clues gathered by using the five senses, focusing on one's feelings and responses in social settings, recalling past occurrences, and actually re-experiencing earlier decisive moments lead to the everyday diagnoses that all people make of themselves and others. The composite or mosaic of these energies makes up how we sense other people, and is symbolized by the egogram.

FOOTNOTES FOR PHILOSOPHERS

1. J. Dusay and R. Poindexter, "How Much Better Are Your Patients?" *TAB*, vol. 4, p. 5, 1965.

2. For a full discussion of the philosophical importance of treatment contracts—see J. Dusay and C. Steiner, "Transactional Analysis in Groups," in *Comprehensive Group Psychotherapy,* ed., H. Kaplan and B. Sadock; Baltimore, Williams & Wilkins, 1971. Note that the TA treatment contracts contain the same elements as legal contracts evolved over hundreds of years—1)

Mutual Assent 2) Competency 3) Legal Object and 4) Consideration.

3. This is the Level Adult Phenomenon, discussed by F. Ernst in *Who's Listening?*, Vallejo: Addresso'set, 1973, Chapter X, pp. 133–152. My wife, Katherine Dusay, was observing me conduct a therapy group in Cochin, India, where language problems were a difficulty. Her observations were presented at the 1st European TA Conference, Villars, Switzerland, July 1975. Instead of listening for words, she observed the eye levels of the participants—an upward gaze was indicative of the Child egostate, a downward gaze indicated the Parent, a straight gaze portrayed the Adult.

4. Karl Abraham contributed a pioneering work (stated in psychoanalytic terms) on the dynamics of how a person's character is related to libido economy, and demonstrated that different types arise from different development periods—"oral," "anal," "pregenital," etc. Written in 1924, his analysis of character types can be found in *Selected Papers on Psychoanalysis, Vol. 1*, New York: Basic Books, 1953.

5. Dr. Frederick Leboyer has provided a refreshing alternative. See *Birth Without Violence*, New York: Alfred A. Knopf, 1975. The effect of treating newborns gently has yet to be realized in Western Civilization.

6. W. Reich, *Character Analysis*, 3rd edition, New York: Orgone Institute Press, 1949 (muscular armoring), and A. Lowen, *Physical Dynamics of Character Structure*, New York and London: Grune & Stratton, 1958 (bioenergetcs), have developed extensive systems of psychotherapy based upon tightness and imbalance in different muscular systems. Ida Rolf, whose work was presented by Andy Crow, November 1974, at the Eric Berne Seminars of San Francisco, has a school of therapy using structural integration—or Rolfing, as it is commonly known—in which physical manipulation of the muscular system is utilized to put the individual back into balance. When this occurs, she finds that neuroses seem to disappear, which leads her.to state: "There is no psychology, just physiology." This position is considered extreme, but it is an important emphasis.

7. When a couple asks, "Are we right for each other?" the marriage counselor may respond with the question, "How does he/she smell to you?"

ANSWER	PROGNOSIS
If both people answer, "Great"	Good prognosis.
If both people answer, "Awful"	Little chance for the union.
If one answers, "Good" and the other answers, "Bad"	Talk to them separately.
If the answer is, "I don't know"	Wait until after six weeks of consultation and ask again.
Or "Are you being serious, Doctor?"	Suggest exercises that increase the Free Child in each of them.

Likewise acupuncturists use smell as one of their diagnostic methods.

8. Konrad Lorenz, *Man Meets Dog,* Harmondsworth, Middx.: Penguin Books, 1953.

9. See the connection of the nose, taste, and their proximity to certain centers of rage, pleasure, appetite, etc.; the anatomical connections have a circle described by Papez. A textbook which has a clear presentation is A. Gatz and F. A. Davis (eds.), *Clinical Neuroanatomy and Neurophysiology,* 4th edition, Philadelphia: 1970. Researchers have shown that certain drugs which effect the emotions also act on these areas.

10. Dr. Louis Thomas, *The Lives of a Cell,* New York: Viking Press, 1974, p. 16. Pheromones are also discussed by B. Patrousky in *Physician's World,* vol. 1, no. 7, July 1973. The olfactory sensation anatomically feeds into the limbic system and the Papez circuit. The origins and importance of smells in psychological affairs are generating some pioneer scientific research. Research on human female vaginal chemistry has been done by R. Michale, and R. Bonsall; see *Science,* vol. 186, no. 4170, p. 1217 (Dec. 27, 1974). Eric Berne, *Transactional Analysis in Psychotherapy,* omitted smell (and taste) in his original list of how to diagnose egostates.

11. A. Comfort, *The Joy of Sex,* New York: Crown, 1972. Finger and toe-sucking have become a current attraction, as described by the noted sexologist Dr. Alex Comfort, who devotes much attention to oral pleasure.

12. This does not mean to imply that all emotion is merely a re-experiencing of the past. Probably most is; however, exaltation and creative joy may be a unique new synthesis.

3

A Sampling of Egograms

Egograms are the psychological equivalent of fingerprints. There are an infinitesimal variety, and no two are exactly alike although they may have certain relationships in common with others. The group of egograms presented in this chapter has been gathered from actual experience to illustrate how character and personality can be understood from their construction.

Two cautions, however, are important in approaching these profiles. One, *observe and gather the data first,* and then construct the egogram; not the other way around. See each person (and yourself) the way he/she really is, and resist the temptation to force him/her into a preconceived notion about his/her character.

Second, "labels" and character types are catchy ways of describing oneself or others at a particular point in time. *Do not settle for a fixed label or category and consider the issue closed.* Labels are helpful in giving a very quick and vivid visual image of someone; however, this should be seen as the beginning, not the end, of the process. The very concept of egograms is that they should be used as a tool in attempting to understand oneself better for the purpose of change and growth.

CRITICAL PARENT TYPES

Those whose predominant egostate is Critical Parent have punitive, fault-finding aspects which limit the creativity of others. But there are positive aspects to this egostate, as to all of the others. Advantages of the Critical Parent are the person's ability to say "No," to stand up for his/her rights and convictions, and to avoid being a patsy. "Stay on the curb!" followed by a strong grip on the little boy, shows how the Critical Parent protects the young offspring's life. Usually, however, when this is the predominant egostate, the personality is experienced as unpleasant and dictatorial (Figure D-1).

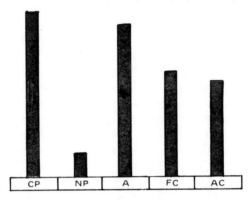

Figure D-1. Tough Cop

Spike, the tough cop, punishes and prosecutes lawbreakers with verve. He is neither lenient nor understanding because his low Nurturing Parent is seldom used. He goes strictly by

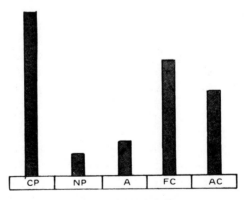

Figure D-2. Criminal

the rules (Adult) and enjoys the excitement of his job (Free Child), but shows little guilt or remorse (lower Adapted Child). If the Adapted Child is higher than the Free Child, then the "tough cop" is more obedient and feels guilty.

This dangerous egogram (Figure D-2) has some similarities to the tough cop, but with an important difference—the criminal does not play by the rules (low Adult). His high Free Child supplies him with creative ideas, but his low Nurturing Parent and low Adult may belie a "crazy killer."

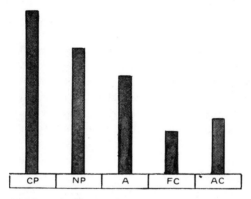

Figure D-3. M.C.P. (male chauvinist pig) or O.F.B. (oppressive female bitch)

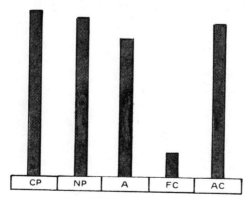

Figure D-4. Marine Sergeant

This type (Figure D-3) forces others into subservient roles by domination and degradation. His/her authority position knows what is best; the Nurturing Parent will care for the followers, but there is no compromise (as evidenced by the low Adapted Child).

The Marine Sergeant (Figure D-4) is tough and rigid, but cares for his own troops (high Nurturing Parent). He doesn't socialize with them, and has a lousy sex life (low Free Child). He salutes his superiors and is obedient to them (high Adapted Child).

NURTURING PARENT TYPES

Nurturing in its most familiar form may be characterized by a loving mother suckling her infant at her breast. Her delight is in watching her healthy, happy children grow and develop. Men exhibit this quality when they are protective, with positive *strokes** and attention. Nurturing individuals feel empathy and understanding for others and tend to use the pronoun "you" more than "I." When these qualities are used to excess, they can inhibit, smother, and drain other people of their confidence and independence.

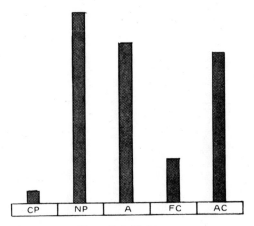

Figure D-5. Big Mama

*See page xviii. This colloquial TA word is gaining popular usage.

This martyr (Figure D-5) is efficient at getting things done (high Adult) and very giving (high Nurturing Parent); yet she has very little fun (low Free Child)—and that's one of the essential features of the martyr position (which explains why she is so big—she raids the refrigerator for self-strokes late at night). Her high Adapted Child goes along with everyone's demands upon her for her time and attention.

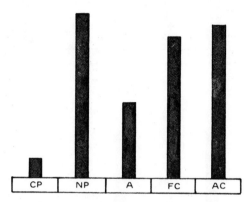

Figure D-6. Soft Sally (Permissive Polly)

Soft Sally (Figure D-6) does everything "right" but no one will listen to her. She has a low Critical Parent. She gets taken advantage of frequently, and usually gives more than she is asked because the word "No" is difficult for her to say to another person.

The Bodyguard (Figure D-7) is faithful and loyal (high Adapted Child); protective (high Critical Parent); and caring (high Nurturing Parent). He is an indebted servant to his employer, and follows directions without thinking (low Adult). He limits his personal pleasure (low Free Child), as his duties always come first.

The Head Nurse (Figure D-8) doesn't stand for nonsense (high Critical Parent), yet is primarily dedicated to helping others (high Nurturing Parent). She immediately takes charge and runs things her way (low Adapted Child), either coercing or nurturing others into compliance. She may be businesslike

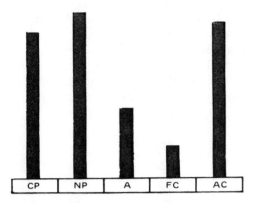

Figure D-7. Bodyguard

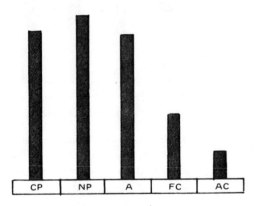

Figure D-8. Head Nurse

with the doctor, as she's figured that's the best way to get things done (reasonably high Adult), and not because she is compromising.

ADULT TYPES

The Adult embodies the qualities of logic and decision making. It is the computer part which adds up bank accounts, figures out gasoline mileage and bus schedules. As it contains no passion, humor, or feeling, the Adult is a dull state at a party, but effective in an accountant's office. It is not to be confused with the "adult" used in the phrase, "Grow up and become an adult." That really means, "Grow up and be an Adapted Child by doing it my way."

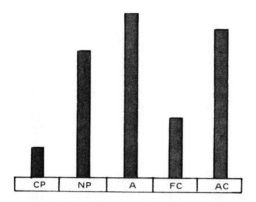

Figure D-9. Good Worker (or Perfect Employee)

This person (Figure D-9) seldom complains about working overtime, is dedicated to the job, and follows directions well (high Adapted Child). High-level thinking would be no problem, and a Good Worker would not say "No" (low Critical Parent), particularly to the boss, so he/she is highly sought after by bosses wishing to have a "yes-man" or "yes-woman."

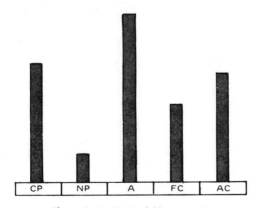

Figure D-10. "No Bedside Manner"

This (Figure D-10) is typical of the surgeon with the "cold heart" (low Nurturing Parent). He/she is great for appendicitis (high Adult), but not much fun for the golf course (low Free Child). This person is sought after when his or her services are needed, yet is generally avoided at social gatherings.

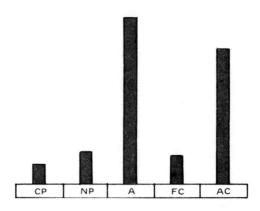

Figure D-11. The Librarian

Commonly known as a bookworm (high Adult), this person (Figure D-11) may be well informed on sexuality and has probably read most of the scientific books on sex (high Adult), but

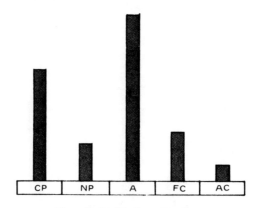

Figure D-12. "No Exceptions"

does little about it (low Free Child). This egogram makes for a knowledgeable librarian or computer operator.

This person (Figure D-12) knows the rules inside and out and goes by them. He would make an excellent door locker at a department store or theater. He lives by the minute hand of the clock, and makes no compromises with late arrivers (low Adapted Child). This exacting loner would be difficult to live with, as he is not interested in being agreeable.

FREE CHILD TYPES

The delightful Free Child is spontaneous, whether he/she is laughing or crying. In him/her rests the basis of intuitive sensing and creativity. The Free Child enjoys sex, freedom, and frivolity. Here lies the similarity between genius and insanity —and also the split between tragedy and comedy. Difficulties arise when the Free Child is out of balance with other parts. Most creative geniuses have a high but balanced (with Adult) Free Child.[1]

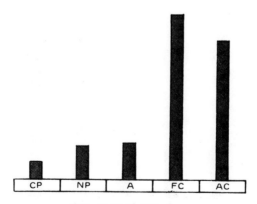

Figure D-13. Thrill Seeker

The Thrill Seeker (Figure D-13) won't say "No" (low Critical Parent) to anything that may be thrilling and bizarre. He/she may use drugs and pleasure-seeking devices of any type without prior thought (low Adult).

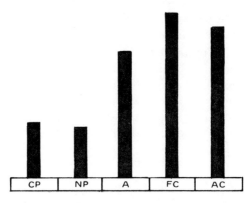

Figure D-14. The Teaser

The Teaser (Figure D-14) sizes up other people accurately (reasonably high Adult) and intuitively (high Free Child), but occasionally detects flaws in others publicly and hurts their feelings. He/she lacks sensitivity to others' sore points (low Nurturing Parent) and is responsible for stimulating misery and self-consciousness in others.

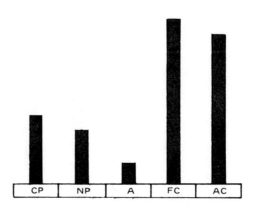

Figure D-15. Starving Artist

This creative soul (Figure D-15) concentrates his/her energies on skills (high Free Child), but won't pay the rent (high Adapted Child). Because his/her reality functioning is minimal (low Adult), he/she may flip out and go crazy.* He/she generally searches for and finds a Big Mama (or Big Daddy).

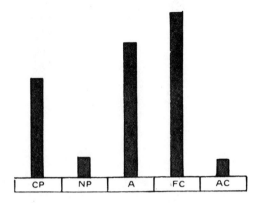

Figure D-16. Don Juan

This "Love 'em and leave 'em" type (Figure D-16) has enough Adult to find love objects, enough Critical Parent to tell them to get lost when he's done, and not enough Nurturing Parent to really care about their feelings. His low Adapted Child prevents guilt feelings and his high Free Child is specifically interested in exciting sexual trysts. (Not exclusively male.)

ADAPTED CHILD TYPES

An Adapted Child is typically compliant, easy to get along with, and usually doing the things he's/she's "supposed" to do, thereby being a submissive, obedient, plastic sort of person. The opposite may also hold true, i.e., the pseudo-rebellious Adapted Child type, who is behaving in an Adapted response to another person by *always* saying "No" to authority or Parent figures (see pp. 52, 198). A compliant Adapted Child compro-

---

*Even though I am a psychiatrist I prefer the terms "flip out" or "go crazy" to more formal terms of psychotic break or schizophrenia for two reasons. First it shows the child-like quality and secondly technical words tend to unfairly label people and be anti-therapeutic.

mises and says "Yes," is eager to please, and easy to live with.
Too much Adapted Child keeps one dependent, however.

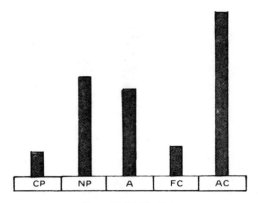

Figure D-17. The Patsy

The Patsy (Figure D-17) works incessantly at pleasing others
and worries a great deal of the time about whether he/she has
done enough (high Adapted Child, low Free Child).[2] He/she
would follow someone "blindly" to the end of the earth as
their psychological slave.

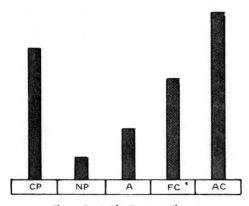

Figure D-18. The Tantrum Thrower

This demanding, insecure Adapted Child (Figure D-18) will insist that his dependency needs are satisfied. He vies for attention at all costs, and loudly protests if he is resisted. An inconsiderate person (high Critical Parent), his conversation is characterized by "me" and "I."

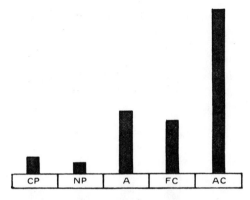

Figure D-19. The Leaner

The Leaner (Figure D-19) is a dependent (high Adapted Child), nonthinking (low Adult) person, who has several needs. He is usually found in a welfare agency or with charitable people. His biggest terror is that he will be rejected or sent away.

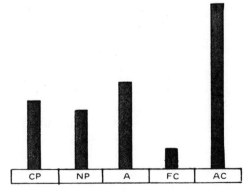

Figure D-20. The Wallflower

The Wallflower (Figure D-20) is a prim and proper person who is completely absorbed in giving others the "right" impression (high Adapted Child). Her morals and values are impeccable, and she has little desire to threaten her untainted purity (low Free Child).

A MIXED VARIETY OF EGOSTATES

When a person has two or more egostates in a high or low position, it may pose certain difficulties or delights. In this mixed grouping, two egostates are usually high, and sometimes equally so, rather than just one predominating egostate as in the preceding section.

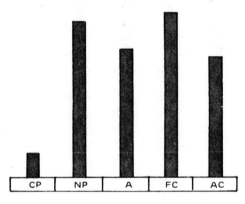

Figure D-21. Cuddle-and-Care

The egogram in Figure D-21 forms the basis for a loving, exciting relationship, full of consideration and robust sex. It ensures a lasting relationship when hooked up with an appropriate person with a complementary egogram. Warmth and romance—the two high areas most frequently sought in long-term relations—predominate.

This self-destructive person (Figure D-22) is angry and hateful (high Critical Parent). His/her wrath is self-directed (high Adapted Child), and there seems to be nothing to live for (low

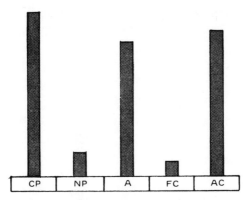

Figure D-22. The Suicide

Free Child). The strong Adult is able to plan and carry out the self-destructive act. The Adapted Child specializes in finding out what is wrong with himself or herself, the Critical Parent has a knack for finding blemishes, and the Adult accurately keeps score.[3]

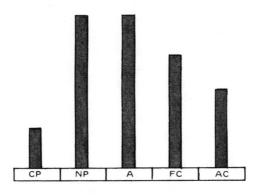

Figure D-23. Guru

The Guru (Figure D-23) is especially interested in making others develop and blossom. Such people exude a high Nurturing Parent, and their strong Adult guarantees that they are good instructors, with a healthy, thoughtful attitude. They may be employed as counselors, program directors, teachers, and other leaders who subjugate their own fun but receive joy by helping others.

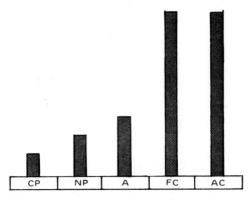

Figure D-24. The Trollop

A fascination for excitement (high Free Child), but with the desire to be protected (high Adapted Child), is the combination in the Trollop (Figure D-24), which results in a love slave. Pleasure and pleasing become the motivations; the other egostates are relatively dormant, since the person doesn't care for his/her partner (low Nurturing Parent), but also doesn't get angry with him/her either (low Critical Parent). Women with this egogram profile sometimes become "kept"[4] and men occasionally become gigolos.

SPECIAL CONSIDERATIONS

In studying what are called mental disorders, particularly "psychosis," egograms give an illustrative approach to what happens functionally. Keep in mind that energies from egostates can flow back and forth from one egostate to another during the process of change (Figure D-25).

During the time of psychosis the Adult may be drained of most of its energy, which goes into the Free Child egostate, accounting for the mystical, bizarre, and occasionally creative

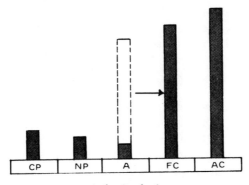

Active Psychosis

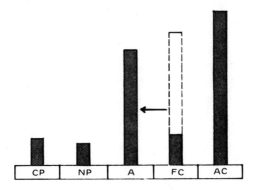

Figure D-25. Convalescent

fantasies. If more of the energy is in the Adapted Child, the behavior is one of withdrawal and usually remorse. On the other hand, if more of the energy is drained into the Free Child, the person may be gleeful and manic, due to the abundance of Free Child.[5] After convalescence, most of the excitement and fantasy from the Free Child drains back into the Adult. A recently "cured," convalescing "psychotic" frequently exhibits a sober Adult, with mechanical and uncontroversial conversation predominating. One reason why people who have flipped out once tend to do it again is because this sober Adult egostate is so boring that the convalescence is intolerable. Much standard treatment of psychosis is directed at suppression of the Free Child and support of the Adult. But a lasting, authentic cure allows both to flourish, rather than stressing one to the exclusion of the other.

ARE MORE CATEGORIES USEFUL?

The fourteenth-century philosopher William of Occam attained notoriety by cutting complicated matters down to their barest essentials. He argued against the Pope and the Church's elaborate and verbose system of faith, which avoided direct sensual experience. He found that word systems (words themselves being abstractions) were superfluous. Occam's statement, "It is vain to do with more what can be done with less," is a maxim that has become known as Occam's razor.[6]

Compatible with Occam's philosophy, egostates have a reality in themselves as they yield direct and certain knowledge. The five categories of egostates are the basic, bare essentials; however, to facilitate further understanding, other categories occasionally can be useful and placed in an egogram. There seldom seems to be any reason for complicating the egogram, although in the Adapted Child there are two distinct possibilities—the *compliant* and the *pseudo-rebellious*. These can be illustrated by Mrs. Clayton and the two men in her life. First, her estranged husband Hugh, whom she loved but could not live with because of his wandering ways and playboy nature. And second, Arthur, a man who was devoted to and somewhat dependent on her. She herself was quite critical of both their behaviors, but had plenty of nurturing left over to take care of these "little boys" in her life (see Figure D-26).

Hugh and Arthur seemed to be quite opposite in their external behavior. One ran away and played; the other stayed behind and absorbed criticism. Their egograms, however, were nearly identical. The difference between them is clarified by separating the Adapted Child into two components: the Pseudo-Rebel and the Compliant. The pseudo-rebellious Child is the part that says "No!" to Mother when she says, "Eat your spinach," and runs away and is argumentative almost in a reflex or habit-like pattern. It is because this is a rebellion in

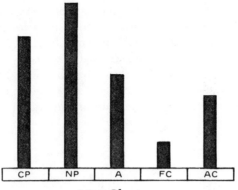

Mrs. Clayton

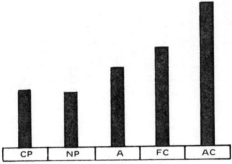

Hugh

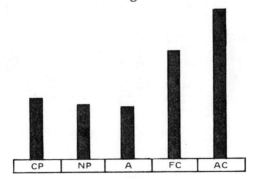

Arthur

Figure D-26.

relationship and reaction to Mother that it is called "pseudo-rebellion." (Authentic rebellion is done more freely, and not in reaction to a parental figure.) The compliant Child, of course, is "Goody Two-Shoes," doing what he or she can to please. Hugh, the playboy, and Arthur, the absorber, become quite different in their personality make-up when looked at with a six-column rather than a five-column egogram (see Figure D-27):

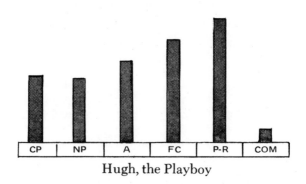

Hugh, the Playboy

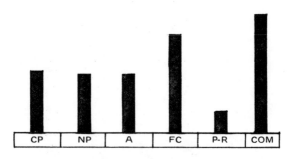

Arthur, the Absorber

Figure D-27. Six Column Egograms

WHAT IS A NORMAL EGOGRAM?

"What's the perfect egogram?" or "What should my egogram be?" are frequent queries. There are no set answers to these questions. Several of the individuals depicted in the preceding sections considered themselves normal, and some of them were happy and content. (Most, however, were not, as these examples were, culled from a clinical experience in which people tended to consult the therapist with complaints of one type or another.) Each of the different personality forces has both its negative and its positive aspects, and it certainly would be unfortunate to have an area in which there was little or no energy at all. On the other hand, if one area totally predominates, lording it over the others in an unbalanced way, then that individual will have a warped personality. Two particular types of egograms are constantly stressed as desirable when people are asked how they would like to be (see Figures D-28 and D-29).

The first is the bell-shaped egogram, in which the Adult is the highest, with the Nurturing Parent and the Free Child flanking in healthy amounts. The second is known as the flat-top egogram, in which a person has an equal amount of all parts.[7] Looking at either of these, one might say, "Well, that looks good to me." That decision is the key. What is desirable lies in the eye of the beholder. Essentially, the question is "How do you want to be for yourself, and what kind of people do you want to be with?" The question of what is or is not normal has really never been resolved, since there is no "normal" egogram in the Bureau of Standards in Washington, D.C.

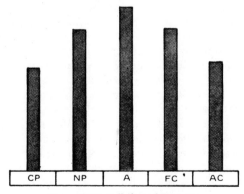

Figure D-28. Bell-shaped Egogram

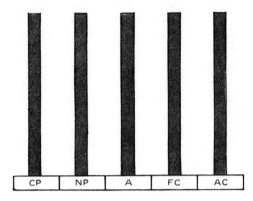

Figure D-29. The Flat-top Egogram

FOOTNOTES FOR PHILOSOPHERS

1. The myth of genius being so close to insanity was explored by Dr. Anne Anastasia, who found that in most respects this was indeed a myth—see her *Differential Psychology,* New York: The Macmillan Co., 1937. It should be noted that some creative genius types, who did *flip out* occasionally, had considerably higher productivity when they were "flipped in"; for example, Vincent Van Gogh did some of his finest painting while recuperating, not while *flipped out.* The incidence of intellectual and emotional disorders is consistently smaller among eminent men and their families than in the general population. In the group studied by H. Ellis, *A Study of British Genius,* London: Hurst & Blackett, 1904, less than 2% had insane parents or offspring, and only 44 cases of emotional disorder were found in a total group of 1030 (only 13 were insane during the active period of their lives; 19 suffered from mild or temporary disorders; and 12 had senile dementia in old age).

2. This profile corresponds to a type of script driver called "Please Me" posited by Dr. T. Kahler and H. Capers in their notion of "Miniscript," *TAJ,* vol. 4, no. 1, January 1974, p. 26.

3. Dr. John Kendra's presentation at the ITAA Annual Summer Conference, San Francisco, August 1973, reported his research findings in which he gathered Rorschach profiles of successful suiciders and/or those who made attempts and he constructed their

egograms. By collating all of these and placing them on a standardized scale, he found that suiciders were extremely low in Nurturing Parent and Free Child; the Nurturing Parent was 7%, the Free Child 3%. The Critical Parent, Adult, and Adapted Child comprised the other 90%; they were nearly equal, with a slight tendency for the Adult to be a little bit lower.

4. Women with an egogram like this get diagnosed in mental health clinics as "hysterics." A classic article by P. Chodoff and H. Lyons, "Hysteria, the Hysterical Personality, and 'Hysterical' Conversion," *American Journal of Psychiatry,* vol. 114, no. 734, 1958, points out these behavioral descriptions of exhibition, sexuality, drama, etc. The diagnosis is applied by male therapists to female patients, indicating that the therapists probably are "turned on" and relieve their anxiety by "diagnosing" the patient.

5. The problem of which egostate feels like the "real self" has been discussed by Berne in *Transactional Analysis in Psychotherapy.*

6. See Bertrand Russell's *Wisdom of the West,* London: Crescent Books, 1959, for a delightful discussion of Occam's philosophy.

7. Heroes in fairy tales and mythology tend to have flat-top egograms. Heroines are quite different; they have an imbalance of high Adapted Child and low Critical Parent. See *Hero In Your Head,* by K. Dusay, Masters thesis, Lone Mountain College, San Francisco, California, 1975.

4

Accuracy of Egograms

HOW ACCURATE IS THE EGOGRAM?

A test or a measurement device is *valid* only if it measures what it says it will. In psychological matters, researchers often deal with things that cannot be weighed, measured by volume or temperature, or tested in a physical sense. Therefore they frequently rely on a mutual agreement among observers. If several trained observers are in accord with each other, there is *consensual validation.*

Dr. George Thomson, a pioneer researcher on egostates, used a tape recorder to preserve nine hours of group therapy sessions. From this tape, he extracted segments whereby each participant appeared for a few seconds to say a couple of words or phrases. When played back, there were varied words, tones, inflections, and volume intensities on each tiny segment. These were presented to a panel of experts in Transactional Analysis for the purpose of differentiating between Parent, Adult, and Child utterances. There was a 95 percent consensual agreement on the egostate classifiations among the panel. These segments were then played to different groups of listeners from various backgrounds, who were requested to identify the egostates they were hearing. The people with no concept about egostate functioning did poorly; however, when they were given some introductory training, they did very well. This demonstrated that egostates exist separately and independently of each other and are readily identifiable entities. They are vital, real, and obvious—not hypothetical constructs of the imagination in the way that Freud's id, ego, and super-ego are. People can quickly spot egostates, classify them, mimic them, and actually improve upon their ability to do so by study and observation. Egostate identification goes far beyond random chance or precocious guessing. The consensual validation of egostates among trained observers yields the building blocks upon which egograms rely.[1]

The original findings which confirmed the validity of egograms took place informally. Five advanced members of a weekly scientific seminar, the San Francisco Transactional Analysis Seminar (now known as the Eric Berne Seminar of San Francisco), were introduced to the concept of egograms, and they enthusiastically volunteered themselves as subjects. Their individual egograms were drawn by fifteen other seminar members who had known them for varying lengths of time. While the fifteen persons drew each subject's personality profile privately, each of the five subjects also drew their own. The result was 100 percent agreement on both the high and low columns of the egograms (although in the case of one drawer who was sleepy and partially intoxicated, the contribution was automatically disqualified).

In various clinical practices, there have been thousands of egograms drawn. When done both intuitively and thoughtfully, agreement among the various drawers reaches 80 to 90 percent. Occasionally, a candidate will try to appear in a way that he/she is not. This is where astuteness and perception come into play on the part of the egogram constructor. In well-trained and advanced groups, there is a high agreement which indicates validity. I have repeated this experiment informally in parties and formally in workshops all over the country, as well as in Europe, Asia, and South America, and have found that the consistency and agreement in egogram construction holds up well under a wide variety of circumstances.

Reliability is also an indispensable criterion of psychological scientists when determining the accuracy of measurements. Reliability infers the ability to repeat the same experiment continually and always come up with the same results. Egograms have been constructed under differing circumstances repeatedly with similar results (this is most often done when clients switch groups, either with the same or different therapists). Hence they are reliable indicators. This finding is often repeated.

The egogram's reliability was originally discovered in a curious way. Camille, an evening TA group member, had her egogram constructed. It portrayed a high Adapted Child and a low Nurturing Parent as the most pronounced features. One of her frequent phrases in the group was, "If you only knew me the way I was *outside* of the group, then you would really know me!" This represented a provocative position on her part, because there is no data, only hunches, about what the person is like in another setting. Her standard statement served to protest against, as well as to discount, others' perceptions about her; it also relieved her of being personally responsible for her behavior within the group. She continually insisted, "I'm really completely different outside of this room (So you can't hold me responsible for my actions in here)." Camille was active in a local singles' group and attended most of their functions. One evening she met a man named Frank, and in their conversation, they discovered that he was in another TA group for which I was the therapist. This coincidence triggered off a revealing episode. In an offhand way, Camille told him, "You know, I feel out of place here. This type of function is just not natural for me. If you could only know me in my usual way, or when I'm in my weekly group and feeling more comfortable, then you'd really know how I am." Frank knew about my penchant for drawing egograms, and on a hunch, he drew Camille's and showed it to me when he came to his next TA group meeting. After his meeting was over, I looked into my desk and found Camille's original egogram constructed weeks before in her own group. Both the way he perceived Camille on the egogram drawn at the party and the one I had previously constructed in my group work with her turned out to be exactly the same. This showed reliably that egograms outside the therapy group are the same as those inside. What is dealt with in the therapy group environment is *real*—a wrestler appears physically strong even if he is seen at the opera wearing a tuxedo. Camille's maneuvers and personality traits came across identically in both places.

Personality traits are visible to an observer who has intuitive awareness. Some people rigidly maintain that you cannot tell what people are really like unless you know them "deeply." These same people are especially vulnerable to con artists. Others who have permission to "see" people the way they really are seldom get "hooked." Of course, when an individual experiences a personality growth, it is reflected by an egogram change. No one in my experience has attained a successful treatment contract without having experienced a valid, reliable energy shift in his/her egogram.[2]

"BOTCHING UP" THE EGOGRAM

When an egogram is erroneously constructed, it is frequently because the individual has not understood the attributes and appearances of the various egostates. This simple lack of information can be rectified by learning and is not a great problem. A more serious way that people can botch up egograms is by playing a psychological game. "Stupid" players lead the parade, as they characteristically have high IQ's but assiduously avoid using their Adult. (Incidentally, it requires huge amounts of energy for bright people to avoid using their Adults.) Even though they catch on to what's happening, they maintain a "Dumb Blonde" or "Mr. Magoo" appearance. "Stupid" players not only forget the simple directions of the egogram; they habitually ask: "What day is it?", "Which bus do I take?", and so on.* An opposite variety from "Stupid," but with similar hallmarks, is the game of "Psychiatry."** Here players exude a profound, professional appearance in which they switch rapidly between different levels of thinking. One

*Groups of mentally retarded children were able to assimilate as well as diagnose according to simple TA concepts.[3]

**Staying on a focused Adult-Adult level is actually *doing* psychiatry, which is to be distinguished from playing it.

"Psychiatry" player may commence by pondering the uncon-scious, while another player discusses here-and-now social be-havior, or may move on to an ethereal or existential viewpoint. Finally, they mix them all together, so ensuring that nothing is either workable or resolvable. (Well-meaning scientists have been observed screaming, hollering, and arguing with one an-other at large international meetings because they were being profound, but unfortunately about different topics at the same time.[4])

"Marshmallow Throwing" is another game which effec-tively botches up egogram construction. A young lady in a group who was adept at this game liked to spar with and delib-erately confront the meaningful people in her life. She particu-larly relished bickering with the therapist over egograms. A new man joined this group and quickly made everyone aware of his presence by exercising his high Critical Parent. He ac-cused some people of being stupid; others he called "sick"; later he proudly described his male chauvinistic attitude to-ward his wife. When his egogram was drawn by the group, "Miss Marshmallow" gave him a miniscule Critical Parent, which was the direct opposite of what all the others had con-structed. When I confronted her with this, she said, "Of course, I knew that everyone was going to draw a high Critical part, so I wanted to toss in something to screw up your sys-tem." She knew that I was experimenting with egograms—basically, she was arguing for the sake of argument. She didn't really want to hurt me, so she tossed a marshmallow which I could easily handle. Her obviously invalid criticism did no harm as she poked in a spot where I (and everyone else in the group) felt confident about our opinions and convictions. There is a clear distinction between "marshmallow throwers" and "rock throwers." A marshmallow thrower criticizes people in their strong areas and doesn't threaten their survival. A rock thrower deliberately aims to attack a person's vulnerable spot, where defenses are weakest. The rock thrower is callous, knows the mark, and hurts the victim.

Being "put on the spot" and forced to show off in drawing an egogram almost always guarantees an inaccurate egogram. The drawer will be put into the self-conscious position of having to perform and make a good impression. The "little professor's" energy rises to the challenge of trying to please someone else while the important faculties become greatly diminished.

"Interference" is a contaminated condition which occurs during delusions, hallucinations, and strong prejudices. Occasionally "psychotic" behavior allows for an uninhibited, vivid, and accurate diagnosis; however there may not be enough Adult present to convey the perceptions either verbally or in writing. Interference can arise from any egostate, but the most frequent and notorious comes from a fixed, rigid Critical Parent. This is viewed as a moralistic person who is admonishing others for being silly and stupid in wasting their energies in a frivolous, unproductive manner. An overworked Adult may even become an interfering culprit by making irrelevant, scientific queries, such as, "Has anyone done a chi-square on this process?"* Any type of interference will mar the construction of a valid egogram.

"Wishful thinking" is another popular bushwacker which frequently occurs when a person is drawing the egogram of a loved one. There is the hidden desire that the paramour will have or will develop more Free Child or Nurturing Parent, and the resultant egogram is a reflection of these hopes. The same thing takes place when a person turns the situation around and draws an egogram of how he/she would like to be rather than perceiving the way he/she really is. Astute observers in a psychotherapy group, or even random acquaintances at a party, can draw more objective egograms of a person than their own husband or wife.

FALSE POSITIVE EGOGRAMS

A "false positive" means that an egogram which was thoughtfully constructed eventually proves to be incorrect. This happens for two reasons. One is that people get confused between what is going on in their heads and what is seen by

---

*A chi-square is a maneuver applied in statistical analysis.

others; and the second is because of a misidentification of ego-states. The person who is drawing his/her own egogram commonly confuses the Critical Parent and the Adapted Child. The Critical Parent, which is seen as tough and demanding on one-self personally, is scarcely noticed by others (see Figure E-1):

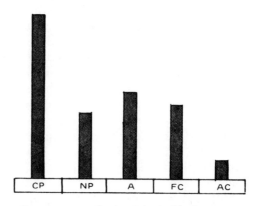

Figure E-1. Example of a "False Positive" Egogram

This person suffered from depressions and angrily berated himself for his weaknesses. He said, "I have a huge Critical Parent; I'm always punishing myself and then I get depressed and feel like an unhappy little boy. That's why I drew my egogram this way." His exterior appearance resembled that of a guilty child who had just been spanked and punished. No one felt criticized or punished *by* him. This was because his critical messages remained hidden inside his head to stage their attacks on him. People viewed him as having a low Critical Parent and a high Adapted Child. His accurate egogram* is seen in Figure E-2.

The Critical Parent and the Adapted Child egostates frequently use identical phrases in their speech patterns. "I hate you," can be the cold, menacing expression of a Critical Par-

---

*Actually, his depressions would probably have subsided were he able to direct his anger outward toward appropriate choices. He set himself up as a person who accepted criticism, so he got it from himself as well as from others.

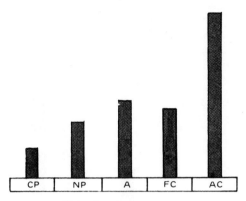

Figure E-2. Correct Egogram

ent, or it can be the words yelled by an Adapted Child writhing on the floor in a temper tantrum. Most nasty name-calling comes from the Adapted Child egostate commonly seen in skirmishes between husbands and wives. This blows over quickly, although the horrendous things said between loved ones (spouses, children, parents, etc.) are shocking when captured on a tape recording and played back later; the same words uttered to a stranger or less familiar acquaintance would result in a poked nose or a lawsuit. When coming from the Critical Parent, however, they do not "blow over." Grudges last for years and become *prejudices* if generalized. Any phrase which is taken out of context may imply several egostates.

A false positive egogram raises the question, "What's going on in my head?" To distinguish inner workings from outward projections, the *psychogram* has been developed.[5] A psychogram portrays what is happening inside a person's head rather than the way he is behaving and being observed by others, and is based on what a person "feels" going on inside. The following example of the egogram-psychogram combination clarifies this distinction (see Figure E-3). It is obvious that the person has a very angry and controlling Critical Parent in his head, which is reflected in his external presentation of the unhappy, guilty, and fearful Adapted Child state. When others see him, as viewed by his egogram, his appearance is that of a very high

Adapted Child and a low Critical Parent. Dreams, fantasies, and self-criticisms are symbolized below the line. Occasionally, double chair techniques and psychodrama (to be discussed later) reveal these inner workings.

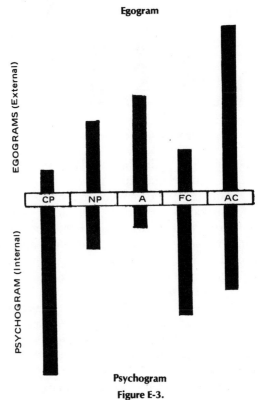

Egogram

Psychogram

Figure E-3.

In the next example, a college student's mother insisted that her son go on to graduate school "for his own good." She maintained that it would be the best thing for him and that she only had his well-being in mind. Her underlying motive could be stated, "If he becomes a professional, he'll make *me* look better. Then I can brag about *my* son's academic success at the weekly bridge parties" (Figure E-4):

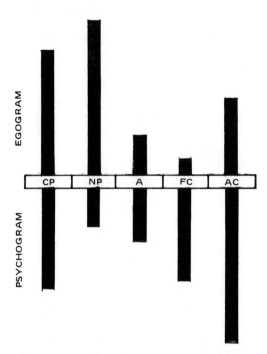

Figure E-4. "Proud" Mother's Egogram and Psychogram

This diagram indicates that in the mother's own head (her psychogram), she is looking for strokes, recognition, and a certain childlike thrill. Her high Adapted Child will be on the alert to inflate itself with strokes usurped from her son's success. Her egogram depicts her as self-sacrificing, caring, and concerned; a mother who is willing to subjugate her own interests for the betterment of her son. There would be no problem if she urged her son to continue his schooling in a straight-forward, uncontaminated way; however, she is receiving personal thrills in a vicarious, surreptitious way. This is not inherently bad but there is danger that she may attempt to influence her son unfairly. On one level, she does not care about his welfare. Her Free Child state (on her egogram) is the lowest, and she might raise it (and also her Adult) by enrolling in school and getting personal strokes for her own achievements. People who live their lives through someone else receive little gratification, recognition, or respect. The quick and effective way to change this is by doing things and initiating projects on their own. Both mother and son gain—and not at the expense of each other.

A psychogram is more difficult to construct accurately, since it deals with a person's own subjective assessment of his/her inner life.[6] It cannot be verified by consensual validation and reliability tests; this is one of its greatest drawbacks and a major reason why I have focused less attention on it.

OTHER ASPECTS

Third Party Egogram

When someone gives pertinent data about an unknown person, only a vague impression of that outsider's egogram can be formed. It may be vastly different from the person's actual egogram. It is common for a therapist to be told about third parties (mates, friends, parents). One teenager recently told me that his mother resembled a cruel, overpowering witch. The woman ultimately visited me and she exuded a cynical, rebellious Adapted Child state. Her cruelty toward her son came from a childlike, teasing state rather than from her Critical Parent. A third party egogram is usually drawn along the lines of "wish fulfillment" from the describer. The person is telling only what he/she wants or imagines the other person to be like; he/she conveniently "forgets" the other characteristics.

Total Picture

The egogram depicts the way a person is seen and sensed at any point in time. It is neither a rapidly fleeting phenomenon nor an assessment of the predominant feature alone. An angry person shaking clenched fists may also have a strong, scientific mind and a loving side. In glancing around an austere funeral parlor, one can sense that certain people are delightful and creative while others are more dull and unimaginative, even though all of them are wearing similar expressions. A person's vibrations and corresponding egogram transcend both the person's mood and temporary situation. When someone refuses to see another person's total picture, it is because he/she wants to fulfill his/her own needs. A Big Mama will look exclusively for the little-boy qualities, dote on these, and discount the other aspects of that person. A playboy type may seek out the sexually curious little-girl parts, thereby ignoring the rest of the lady he encounters. These seekers are in for a surprise when they are attacked by the previously ignored parts. (He/She wasn't that way when I met her" is commonly heard in marriage counselors' offices by persons who erased or overlooked certain incompatible parts of their love object.)

Dreams

One evening, a gentleman told his therapy group about a vivid dream he had had. The group decided to construct this man's egogram based exclusively on the dream information. The egograms came out random, without any uniformity. The reason for this is because a dream state is a total manifestation of the Free Child, creative in both its content and presentation. One would be diagramming a translation of the creative aspects of the dreamer. Similarly unreliable results may occur from drawing egograms of painters or writers by their canvases or their novels (i.e., a wild sexual tale may be written by a person who is externally inhibited). Adult analysis would be incomplete.[7]

Age Validity of Egograms

Drawing an egogram of young children is haphazard and incomplete because they mainly exhibit their active Free Child or perhaps their patronizing Adapted Child side. Fledgling elements of the Parent may be present and certain predictions may be made, but a child's egogram remains in the realm of guesswork. Certain predictions about what the child will be like may be formulated by viewing the parents who are shaping and contributing to this child's personality. Nonetheless, the egogram constructions of children under six have been random and unpredictable. Until the age of eleven, the child does not have a fully developed Adult, nor are the Parent parts consistent because the values are in a state of flux.[8] Therefore egograms are not generally done on children under the age of eleven. Teenagers portray more definite and valid egograms; but ideally, the most consistent egogram work will result when it is being used by people over eighteen years of age.

Conducive Atmosphere

A friendly, open environment, as contrasted to a solemn, hardworking atmosphere, is a prerequisite for intuitive functioning. Psychotherapy groups, as well as social groups, vary in their moods and tones. Some are predominantly Free Child —filled with laughter and spontaneity. Some are sober Adult gatherings with direct questions and scientific responses. Parental groups focus upon nurturing and congratulating, or confronting and criticizing. Groups which contain various mixtures of the egostate elements exhibit spontaneity, growth, and the necessary components to construct egograms. It has been popular for some people to present egogram drawing sheets with the percentage marks already filled in. Unfortunately, this places too much Adult attention on percentage construction and decreases the Free Child intuitive attributes.

Mate Choice

Friends, lovers, enemies, even psychotherapy groups are chosen by persons who base decisions on their own primitive egogram perceptions. Random chance is not involved. People who have decided to feel bad easily team up with those who are adept at criticizing. Then it is easy for them to get kicked, yelled at, or put down. This explains the common hook-up of the "Kick Me" player and the "Now I've Got You, You Son of a Bitch" player. Coupling is the end result of people who are searching for positive and rewarding experiences, as well as for those who are seeking the opposite. Both types find their mates with ease. An egogram match of a couple gives insightful information, particularly in answering the question, "Is this the right person for me?" This is done by placing each partner's egogram on top of the other and comparing them, paying special attention to the states they have in common (see Figure E-5):

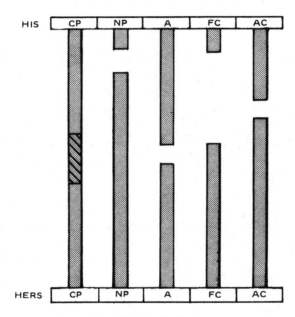

Figure E-5. Couples Egogram

A couple's egogram exposes differences and similarities. In the egogram mold above, presented by Dr. S. Karpman, with the man on top and his partner below, it is apparent that there are varying gaps between some egostates and a predominant area of overlap.[9] (The same scale must be used when drawing a couple's egogram. The importance of combined egograms is discussed in Chapter Nine.)

The important symbiotic or mutually dependent relationship between a mother and her baby has been elucidated by E. Schiff, who depicted their combined relationship with a composite egogram graph (see Figure E-6):

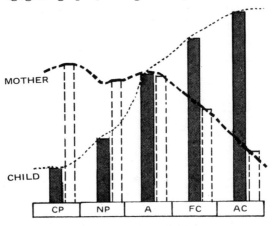

Figure E-6.

The symbiosis breaks down at the point where the curves overlap; in this example, it dissolves when mother and child are both in the Adult egostate. (Symbiosis is a normal condition in early child development, but later leads to pathology and decreases more independent thinking.)[10]

Friends and Other Enemies

Occasionally, persons who are termed enemies have dramatically similar and complementary personalities. Two opposing military generals from warring nations can have nearly identical egograms, and probably do.* They would certainly understand each other, might share similar tactics and philosophies, and under different circumstances, might be close friends and drinking buddies. However, each general would have a vastly different egogram from a fellow citizen of his nation who was a war resister with a different belief system. Radical political

---

*Unfortunately, this remains speculation as no two wartime generals have had their egograms compared, and their personality diagnosis comes from biographies—risky at best.

right-wingers and radical left-wingers have similar personality traits and nearly identical egograms, although they view each other as the hated enemy. Like the two opposing war generals, they share a certain psychological kinship. An egogram was drawn of a tough, right-wing, law-and-order type, and it showed a high Critical Parent and low Adapted Child. A nearly identical egogram was constructed of a radical left-wing revolutionary leader (see Figure E-7):

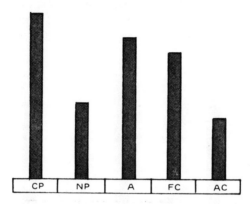

| CP | NP | A | FC | AC |

Figure E-7. Right-Winger and Left-Winger Egograms

With this combination, each leader feels that he/she is right and the other person definitely wrong. Each uses the high Critical Parent with its self-righteous position to arrive at this conclusion. Their Adapted Child was minimal, illustrating the fact that they were unwilling to reach a compromise. Instead, they remained strong-willed and biased in their individual yet contrasting propaganda (different lyrics to the same tune). Neither chose to listen, compromise, tolerate dissidence, nor accept leadership from others. This explains why the day after a successful revolution, the victorious revolutionary becomes a strong, conservative dictator.*

---

*This is also true for the mythological hero—to remain a hero, he must die before he has a chance to become an oppressor: "The hero of yesterday becomes the tyrant of tomorrow unless he crucifies *himself* today"—Joseph Campbell, *Hero with a Thousand Faces.*

Group Egograms

"I don't want to go to that party because they are a bunch of fuddy-duds"—in this case, an entire group of people's general impressions are being diagnosed and commented upon. A so-called hippie, just released from police headquarters where he had been taken on suspicion of carrying marijuana, says to his friend lazing in the sunshine: "Man, those were bad vibes in there." This statement visually depicts the forces sensed in the way the hippie viewed the police. An undercover agent goes back to his superior to report on the underground party he attended and comments, "That group was really weird!"

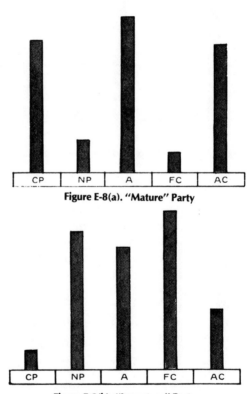

Figure E-8(a). "Mature" Party

Figure E-8(b). "Immature" Party

A person who is caught in an uncomplementary group flounders like a fish out of water. If given the choice between a "mature" or an "immature" party on Friday night, the fun-lovers will smile and dash off to their chosen party. The egograms of the mature and immature parties in Figures E-8(a) and E-8(b) reveal their differences.

The "mature" group is very concerned with being grown-up, proper, and dignified. Each participant is concerned about making a good impression. At social functions, this group egogram would predictably ensure that defensive behavior would be interlaced with caution and coyness. Perhaps insults and derogatory remarks would ensue, interspersed with brilliant Adult assessments. The minimal appearance of the Nurturing Parent and the Free Child would guarantee a lack of understanding and fun. The immature party on the other hand, as depicted by its egogram, would consist of warm, friendly, happy people who have gotten together for a good time and some pleasant experiences. Group egograms can be drawn of religious societies, cities, organizations, and nations.[11] Perhaps different cities' skylines are a reflection of their egograms (see Figure E-9).

Now that you have seen a fresh way to view yourself and others, what follows are ways to grow and change. Part II tells what you can do about your egogram (personality).

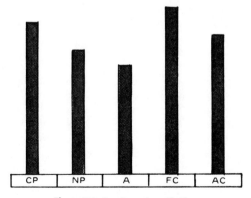

Figure E-9. San Francisco Skyline

FOOTNOTES FOR PHILOSOPHERS

1. George S. Thomson, "The Identification of Egostates," *TAJ,* vol. 2, no. 4, October 1972, pp. 196–211; Thomson noted that the ability of a "schizophrenic" and a "depressive" patient to iden- tify the Parent egostate was markedly decreased from "normal" people. See also J. Hurley and H. Porter, "Child Egostates in the College Classroom," *TAB,* vol. 6, no. 2, January 1967, p. 28. In this experiment, the egostate compilations were compared to var- ious tests: the MMPI Psychopathic Deviate Scale, the Marlowe- Crowne Social Desirability (SD) Scale, the true-false version of LaForge's Interpersonal Check List (ICL), and the scores on the Orthogonal Factors (LOV and VOM). The results indicated that, sure enough, the Adapted Child was linked with the lower psy- chopathic deviants and lower dominating factors (which reflect rebellious and dominating tendencies), but had a much higher SD and LOV score (these reflect the conforming and acceptance tendencies). This, of course, indicates actual measurements of egostates.

2. At the present time, I am maintaining clinical research into (1) whether or not a client gets what he/she consulted me for (i.e., attaining the TA contract); and (2), whether or not he/she had a shift in the egogram. So far there is a strong positive correlation between the two factors. (A few people did shift egograms but have not attained their contract yet, but not vice versa.) The egogram may serve as a test instrument to resolve a difficult research problem in psychotherapy—whether or not someone actually got better.

3. This is a personal report from workers at Sonoma State Hospital in California.

4. Berne, *What Do You Say After You Say Hello?,* pp. 409–413.

5. The psychogram, a currently popular term in Californian TA circles (cf. Del Casale's "endogram" in the next footnote), is self- recognized and is not a formal research tool like an egogram because it cannot be observed and validated by outsiders. This raises once again questions about the dynamic unconscious. Is our behavior determined by active inner forces that are hidden from our awareness—the Freudian theory? Or is our behavior controlled by conscious, albeit habitual, decisions—an idea which currently appeals to me? Different possibilities exist as to how much importance to place on inner contents of the head:

a. Are "inner" (hidden) forces of the same intensity as "outer" observable forces—the egogram being identical to the psychogram?

b. Is there some inverse relationship between inner forces and outer, i.e., high inner Critical Parent = high outer Adaptive Child? Del Casale possibly has some evidence for this gathered from psychodrama techniques.

c. Is there no relationship at all between inner and outer forces?

d. Are there no inner forces at all??

When a student sheds cherished assumptions, these possibilities become exciting.

6. The endogram concept of Dr. Francisco Del Casale, an internist from Buenos Aires, was formally presented at the Eric Berne Seminar of San Francisco in August, 1974. A. Rissman of San Francisco, also presenting at the same seminar, has developed a model for clarifying inner dialogue called the "trilog." The psychogram seems to be the energy model corresponding to the trilog (*TAJ*, vol. 5 no. 2, April 1975, p. 170), whereas the egogram corresponds to transactional and game diagrams. Although I originally supported the terminology, it now seems that the same words for inner dialogue, i.e., Parent, Adult, and Child, are a misnomer; probably egostate precursors would be more appropriate.

7. Dr. Paul Federn—*Psychiatric Quarterly*, vol. 31, 1957, pp 681–689—an early member of the Vienna Psychoanalytic Society, realized that neurotic traits could be detected by the style of writing due to incomplete repression in psychoanalytical terms. Translating this into TA language, it is because "neurotic" traits are lodged both in the Adapted Child and the Free Child's uncontrolled fantasies. Whenever the fantasies are committed to the written word, the Adult part becomes involved.

8. Jean Piaget found that a human being is unable to hypothesize before the age of eleven.

9. Dr. S. Karpman has drawn an interesting analysis between couples' compatibility by using the couples' egogram—*TAJ*, vol. 4, no. 4, October 1974, p. 16. These different egostate positioning areas have different meanings. An area of overlap indicates compatibility, and the area with the greatest differential margin depicts where most game playing comes from. Married couples will not remain together unless they have at least two areas of overlap or confluence (J. Dusay, 1973, Presentation at Eric Berne

Seminars of San Francisco). It is easy to spend an evening with an individual with whom you have only one area of overlap (usually sexual, sometimes academic); but it is difficult to spend a lifetime with a person with whom you have only one primary element in common. People tend to hook up with others who have similar egograms which will interdigitate and fit with their own (see Chapter 9).

10. E. Schiff, *TAJ*, vol. 4, no. 4, October 1974, p. 13.
11. Scott Wichman, an astute psychiatric technician, came up with these findings in a large metropolitan clinic.

PART TWO

EGOGRAMS IN CHANGE
AND GROWTH

5

The Elements of Change

People devote tremendous energy to the continual flow of decision-making processes: "Should I eat now?", "Where?", "Do I look OK?", "Shall I buy this pair of shoes?", "Should I speak to him?", and on and on until bedtime. Occasionally the forces of one egostate may oppose another in conflict; for instance, the Child may say, "I want to," and the Parent may respond, "You can't." The opposite situation occurs when the Parent says, "You should," and the Child responds, "I don't want to." The Adult egostate serves a valuable purpose in these disagreements and when activated it is a mediator. Through the Adult, resolutions and compromises are made. Sometimes one or more of the person's egostates are both powerful and stubborn and will not consult with the Adult. When this happens, the decision-making ability is impaired.

The elements involved in a behavior change are illustrated by the following case of Judd, who was diagnosed as a hypochondriac by the innumerable physicians who treated him before he was referred to me. He complained about being weak, weary, headachey, and jittery as he displayed his collection of pills and remedies, and was distinctly annoyed with doctors who could not find anything physically wrong with him. Judd's belief that he was sick was seen to reach far back into his past as he nostalgically reminisced about his family's medicine cabinet, and remembered his mother taking his temperature and giving him an assortment of pills. He loved visiting his family physician as well as the neighborhood pharmacy.

Judd clearly received psychological strokes from his mother for being a weak, sickly child.

Judd was able to repeat his early lifestyle with his wife, who was similar to his mother. They both had a high Nurturing Parent as well as a high Adapted Child in their personality constructions. His wife nursed ailing Judd with medicines and potions, and they shared a "comfortable relationship." I invited him to join my transactional analysis group, and at the first session the group members drew his egogram (see Figure F-1):

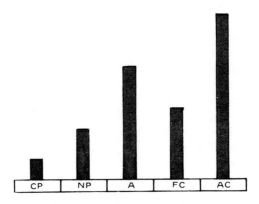

Figure F-1 Judd's Egogram (Before TA)

SURFACING THE CHILDHOOD DECISIONS

Judd's high Adapted Child in his egogram is what shows up in the here-and-now as he insists he is sick—and habitually thinks, feels, and behaves as a weak, sickly person. The origin of this personality trait was uncovered in the following manner.[1]

One evening, Judd remarked to the group that his wife insisted that he take pills, and a group member piped up, "Why don't you stop paying attention to her?" Judd looked helpless and replied that he was "afraid" to argue with her, feeling that it was more comfortable to agree. Judd appeared to be upset and I asked what was troubling him. He said that whenever he was asked to do things, he felt sick. I asked him to recall a specific incident of this and Judd brought up a situation that happened only a few days before. His wife complained that the garage mechanic had not tuned up the family automobile properly and urged him to return it personally and demand better service. Judd agreed with her argument, but he soon developed a splitting headache and was "unable" to carry out the task.

In order to get a clearer picture of what was going on in Judd's head, I asked him to close his eyes and imagine that it was last Saturday morning again. When he was "back in the scene," he was instructed to open his eyes and pretend that his wife was sitting in an empty chair which I had placed directly in front of him. I then directed him to begin speaking to his wife in the present tense, as if the scene was happening right then and there in the group.

JUDD (playing himself): "What a beautiful morning! I'd like to sit around and relax all day."

To create a replay of forces involved in the struggle, I directed Judd to switch places and become his wife.

JUDD (playing his wife): "The mechanic didn't fix our car—take it back and stand up for our rights—do something about it!"

Whether or not his wife said those exact words is not important. What is important is that Judd "felt" this type of pressure from his wife. He then switched to his original chair and answered his wife's statements.

JUDD (playing himself): "I'm feeling scared now (but I don't want to tell her that). My head aches and I'd better stay home and rest."

Judd was *role-playing* a scene in which he felt scared and then sick. Knowing that these day-to-day occurrences are reflections of deep inner conflicts in a person's life, I went on to ask him if he felt this way often. He replied that he had—most of his life in fact. This was not uncommon. People frequently maintain negative feelings such as being sad, mad or scared throughout their lives. Perhaps at one time these feelings may have been appropriate for earlier experiences, but later they become what are called habitual "rackets" i.e., inappropriate ways of feeling. Because of this, we proceeded to trace Judd's feeling back to original experiences, looking for ones that triggered Judd's negative and self-defeating response. Judd was again asked to close his eyes and remember other times in his past when he felt sick. Judd first recalled incidences from his more recent past but then began to dip further and further back into his memory. He paused at similar events in his young adult life, college, high school, and grade school days, and finally arrived at what he considered to be his earliest memory about feeling scared and sick. This earliest-recalled feeling experience is what I term a "prototype episode." Rather than debate whether or not he could go "further" or provide more information, I accepted these consciously recalled "feeling" memories because they were and are distinct and workable.[2] The group provided a nurturing attitude combined with logical thinking, and Judd accepted our permission actually to be in that early situation and re-experience the feelings through talking about them out loud to us. This is the process known as *surfacing* whereby a person externalizes and verbalizes archaic hidden inner feelings. Judd began to quiver and said, "I'm five years old, and I want my mommie to come to nursery school with me, but she won't. Please Mommie, I'm not big enough. I'm scared . . . I'm sick!" Judd had beads of sweat on his forehead and began to rub his stomach. I told him to place his fantasized "Mommie" in the empty chair in front of him and tell her what he was feeling.

JUDD (being age five): "I'm scared. My tummy aches and my head aches, and I want to stay home with you."

He was then told to switch places with his "Mommie" and answer little Judd.

MOMMIE (as played by Judd): "I know you don't feel very good, so let me give you some pills for your head and tummy and then you can go to school."

I continued to direct this dialogue between five-year-old Judd and his "Mommie," and it went like this:

JUDD: "I feel so sick. I don't think the medicine will help."

MOMMIE: "Well then, I'll put you back to bed now, and I'll give you some pills, and by tomorrow, you'll feel good enough to go to school."

JUDD (very relieved): "Okay. If I'm sick and stay home, at least I won't be so scared."

I interrupted Judd and asked, "What are you deciding about yourself now?" He replied, "I'm scared of people. I'm scared of going to school and being with the other little boys. If I stay sick I won't have to face them."

Judd's real mother, for her own psychological reasons, was nervous about having a healthy child who could someday leave her. She passed her anxiety and scared feelings on to Judd by the scripting process illustrated in Figure F-2:

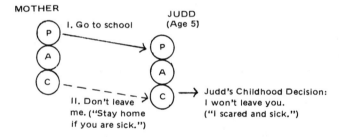

Figure F-2. Judd's Script (developed by age five)

The solid arrow (I) from Mother's Parent to Judd's developing Parent egostate ingrains in him the value of "Go to school," which is expressed later in life as, "Go out and be productive, be a man," etc. The dotted line (II) from Mother's Child egostate to Judd's Child egostate represents the incompatible injunction, "Don't leave me!"—and Judd is fearful of going away from his mother. After hundreds or perhaps thousands of these injunctions, the Child in Judd (the Adapted Child) finalized his decision and agreed with Mother's nervousness, "I'm scared too—I won't leave (I'll be sick instead)." This is the basic childhood decision which he carried with him through his life, right into my office. That's why the doctors who had told him, "It's all in your head," were ineffectual. They assumed that they were talking to a logical forty-year-old man, whereas a five-year-old child was actually running the show. In treatment, I have found that dealing with a person's early feeling experiences is more fruitful than spending endless hours, months, or even years trying to come up with many intellectual tidbits about a person's early "trauma."

Judd was encouraged to re-experience this "little-boy" ego-state feeling and express it fully. We specifically did not pressure him to be grown up at that phase of treatment. By surfacing his early feelings and thoughts, Judd was then able to view the original scene that set the tone of his life. I crystallized his script message by repeating what Judd had himself discovered.[3] He was reassured that being a five-year-old little kid really was scary; when his mother worried about him, he worried about himself too and was afraid to go out and play with the other little boys and girls. When it came time to go to school, it was even more scary and the only way for him to really keep his "Mommie" around was to be sick. For Judd, the TA group provided a safe milieu for re-experiencing important moments in early childhood. This in itself provides relief for most people. However, surfacing and re-experiencing decisive childhood feelings is certainly not the final point of change-oriented treatment.

REDECISION

To change, one must *redecide.* I told Judd, "I see that you're scared, but you've really done some very strong work to arrive back at the early time in your life when you decided this." I then reintroduced Judd to his other powers by focusing on the other forces represented in his egogram—his logical and scientific part (the Adult); the Free Child spirit of joy and life; and the Nurturing Parent where he is willing to take care of himself to promote growth. I asked him, "Are you willing to open your 'scared' little boy to your other parts?" and he said, "I'm willing to have a go at it."

In my experience, no one is fixed, or totally sick, or scared, or whatever they feel about themselves. All people have positive forces that can oppose the scripted parts and somehow arrive at a *solution* for changing the course of their lives (see Figure F-3):

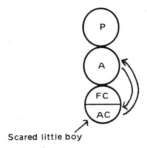

Scared little boy

Figure F-3. Redecision Structure

Judd's cure came from inside his own head—I have represented it by the arrow from his Adult to his Adapted Child. His Adult was chosen to oppose his scripted Adapted Child because this logical force was quite strong in him; however, other egostates such as Nurturing Parent and Free Child may be equally or even more effective in the redecision process.*

During the course of treatment, Judd regained his own power and responsibility for controlling and directing his life. When he decided to take charge of his own thinking and feeling faculties, he was ready to make a redecision about the course his life would take. To facilitate his redecision, a conversation between his weak, conforming part (Adapted Child) and his scientific, rational part (Adult) was structured. Again, I asked him to switch chairs as he switched egostates. This "spatial" separation helped him to distinguish between differing forces in his head. With these two egostates out in the open, Judd was prepared to confront and adjust his initial decision

---

*R. Goulding has found that the spirit of life which is characteristic of the Free Child is specially important in reversing suicide feelings.

about life. I catalyzed this interaction by directing him to switch egostates at the appropriate times.[4]

JUDD (Adapted Child): "I feel sick and I'm scared to go to school by myself."

JUDD (Adult): "Why are you scared?"

JUDD (Adapted Child): "Because I'm afraid I'll get lost and I can't take care of myself."

JUDD (Adult): "Little five year olds can't take care of themselves."

JUDD (Adapted Child): "I know! I'm so scared and I think my stomach hurts."

JUDD (Adult): "You said you *think* your stomach hursts?"

JUDD (Adapted Child): "Well, it kind of hurt, and my mother thinks it hurts."

JUDD (Adult): "Do you think you might have talked yourself into this?"

JUDD (Adapted Child): "Yes, I think so. My stomach doesn't hurt me any more than anyone else's stomach hurts, but it helps me forget about my scare."

JUDD (Adult): "How long do you want to keep scaring yourself and having stomach aches?"

JUDD (Adapted Child): "No longer. I don't have anything to be scared of. I can take care of myself now. I'm not so little any more".

I stopped Judd's conversation and asked him how he felt. He said he felt great, as if he were healthy for the first time in his life—he no longer was dominated by the little boy in his head. Others in the group were very happy for him and freely gave him hugs and congratulations.

No doubt many people make major redecisions in life without turning to formal psychotherapy. My hunch is that these same processes of recognizing primary episodes, surfacing the feelings, and then applying one's own positive personality forces are commonly in operation in most people as they live their lives. When people find that they are "stuck" and won't let go of old habitual feelings or "rackets," they may very wisely seek help from others. In our groups we support growth processes and provide the milieu for change, but we do not rob people of their own power and potency by telling them what to do—ultimately they tell themselves.

SLIPPAGE (INTERNAL RESISTANCE)

Unfortunately, in my experience, the process of redecision and the corresponding personality change has rarely proceeded in such a straightforward and simple manner as Judd's example.[5] If it did, the process of gaining personal freedom would be easy. Something usually happens to botch up the simple flow by which present-day reality (Adult) or caring (Nurturing Parent) or creativity (Free Child) deals with past traumas and unfortunate childhood decisions (Adapted Child). Many different psychiatrists and theorists have coined various terms which they use to describe how people block their normal growth.[6] These have been called "resistances," "defenses," sometimes "impasses," and other things. The term that I have chosen is "slippage"—implying a very specific happening. Slippage is when an individual, attempting to apply his/her Adult egostate to the scripted, Adapted Child part in his/her head, shifts energy from the Adult into some other egostate—usually the one that is highest on his/her egogram (or next to the highest).* This is in conformity to the principles of resistance demonstrated in Chapter Six (pp. 102 and 105-106).

We will now detour from Judd's successful resolution to demonstrate how he could have ruined his development by slippage.

JUDD (Adapted Child): "I am weak."

THERAPIST. "Switch to your Adult in the other chair."

JUDD (Phony Adult): "Will you try to look at why you think you're weak?"

This is labeled a Phony Adult rather than Adult because the words are already giving permission to do nothing—a pleading "will you try" is vastly different from a "Do it" attitude (nonverbal clues such as upward voice inflection and a raised brow also are heard and seen). This slippage proceeds:

JUDD (Adapted Child): "I think I'm weak because my mother took me to the doctor a lot."

*I do not mean to imply that the Adult egostate is the exclusive curative force. Any egostate may be curative depending on the existential position of the client.

THERAPIST (Phony Adult): "That's interesting. Tell me more."

JUDD (Adapted Child): "And furthermore, I think that I am in a bad position because I've taken a lot of medicine and things and I can't seem to find anything else."

JUDD (Phony Adult): "Hmmm, that's interesting. You must have had all sorts of things going on inside of you."

JUDD (Adapted Child): "Yes, I did. Let me tell you some more."

JUDD (Phony Adult): "That's interesting. Go on, tell me some more."

This is an illustration of a functional impasse in Judd. When Judd switched to the supposed Adult Chair, he slipped very rapidly into his Adapted Child. This sounded like two children playing Psychiatry, having what was known as an interesting discussion, which could drag on and on without any confrontation or thrust toward redecision (Perls called this "head tripping"). Because of his overbalanced Adapted Child as seen on his egogram, Judd's natural tendency was to go in that direction. Slippage, however, can actually occur from any of the other egostates, most commonly the Critical Parent. The following is an example of slippage into the Nurturing Parent, chosen to show that the Nurturing Parent, usually regarded as a positive force, may impede growth. The use of different chairs very clearly demonstrated the slippage which was in the open where it could be seen and confronted.

JUDD (Adapted Child): "I am weak."

JUDD (in his supposed Adult seat, but beginning to slip): "It would be helpful if you would go ahead and tell me where this all started."

JUDD (Adapted Child): "I was young when it happened."

JUDD (definitely slipped into Nurturing Parent): "I'll try to help, so go ahead and express those feelings."

JUDD (Adapted Child): "I really feel bad; I really feel weak."

JUDD (more blatantly Nurturing Parent): "You should really go ahead and experience those feelings. It's good for you."

JUDD (Adapted Child): "Oh, it really hurts, I really feel . . ."

JUDD (supposed Adult, but actually Nurturing Parent): "That's good for you, you'll feel a lot better expressing your feelings; things will be a lot better and you won't ever feel bad again."

Instead of Adult logic being applied, reassurances are offered. Nurturing oneself is not inherently disastrous. Usually it feels good; yet overnurturing may smother change. Judd was rescuing himself and providing false reassurances which he did not trust, and which he had heard before many times. This tended to keep him in his Adapted Child position functionally, rather than providing him with Adult information that could be evaluated. In the original example, when Judd proceeded very quickly to the resolution, it was seen that he stayed in his Adult and a solution was forthcoming. When slippage did occur, first into the Adapted Child when he played "Psychiatry" rather than providing a straight Adult confrontation, and then in the second example into the Nurturing Parent, as he gave himself false reassurances, the group members confronted him about the shift.

Although the above illustrations were rather blatant, slippage is usually pretty subtle, seen most often in body postures or hidden gestures. The very reason that Judd had not solved his problems alone by his own thoughts was either because of his inability to see himself accurately or his unwillingness to confront himself. (This is why doing double chair work at home alone seldom works.)

A useful method for correcting slippage is facilitated by introducing a third or "perpendicular" chair to bring back the Adult. Judd had slipped into his Nurturing Parent egostate while sitting in the supposed Adult chair, by telling himself that he "should" express his feelings and that "everything would be OK" if he did, so I took a third chair and placed it in a perpendicular position from which the other two could be observed. At this point, I reintroduced Judd to his Adult and said, "Judd, come over to this chair here that I have provided." Judd came over, sat down, and the dialogue went like this:

THERAPIST: *"Describe* what is happening between these two people." (I pointed toward the two empty chairs that he had just vacated.)

JUDD (Third Chair): "Well, it looks like the little boy is doing his thing, and when I was in the Adult chair, I started to nurture and come on like my mother used to."

THERAPIST: "What do you make out of that?"

JUDD (Third Chair): "Well, really, I wasn't Adult, I was Parent."
THERAPIST: "How does that go?"
JUDD (Third Chair): "Slow. It looks it could go on forever."

By sitting in a third chair, Judd was able plainly to see what was going on inside his head—a Parent/Child dialogue. From this position he was able to "think" things over and perceive what was blocking his ability to change. Consequently he attained the necessary distance to see himself objectively. From his third chair (Adult) he turned to the empty chair representing the Nurturing Parent and said, "Would you be willing to knock off 'helping' the little boy so that he can figure out things for himself?" Judd spontaneously switched to the Nurturing Parent chair and replied, "I believe little Judd is weak and always needs me—but I'll let him alone for a while."

This use of the perpendicular chair halted the slippage and enhanced a return to Adult control. In addition to myself, the other group members served as Adult consultants and more importantly, shared their own feelings with Judd from their other egostates. Occasionally the slippage or impasse persists after a third chair is added. When this happens, I have found it advantageous to back off for a while and give the person some time to assimilate what has occurred.

PRACTICE

Beyond the confines of the group treatment setting, but just as important, is the necessity of *practice*. This means putting one's new attitudes into action. Whenever someone regards the work done in a treatment session as the definitive task, they are kidding themselves and will likely relapse back into old behavior. It does very little good to either make a redecision or to "catch on," and then do nothing more about it.

The two most important mottos in authentic action are: (1) *Do something different,* even though it *doesn't feel right;* and (2) It's OK to change, get better, and *find out why later.* These simple mottos have profound underpinnings and they confront the two greatest copouts of our era. The "feeling" copout, as in "I would do it but it doesn't feel right," and the "thinking" copout, in "I would change if only I could understand." When people polarize and cling to either their thinking or their feeling aspects, stagnation results. The antithesis is for "thinkers" to feel more and for "feelers" to think more.

Judd decided that he would be OK, not be scared, and thought that getting into good shape physically would be helpful for him to reinforce his new, healthy viewpoint of himself. He made a commitment to himself (shared with others) that he would practice jogging, even though it did not "feel right." This practice of new actions enlarged the structure necessary for these very actions.[7] He worked up to jogging 2 miles a day and exercised at the local gym. His legs and lungs felt better regardless of where he went and his craving for cigarettes diminished and eventually disappeared. He even admired his new jogging shoes like they were a new toy. His wife adjusted her morning schedule and ultimately enjoyed getting up early with him; Judd waved at the newspaper boy each morning as he jogged around the corner and later, at the office, his business associates told him how healthy he looked. He chose a new set of office friends to lunch with and enjoyed conversations about nourishing foods and invigorating sports. Judd admitted that he did not miss his old martini-drinking lunch hours. Another jogger and he became good friends and, finally, he won a trophy in the over-forty running club. The structures in his life, all the way from his musculature to the institution at which he worked, supported his new behavior. This, however, did not evolve without a struggle. Predictably there are resistances to change all along the route.

OVERCOMING EXTERNAL RESISTANCE

This new position in life was not automatic after Judd decided to "be strong" in his head. In addition to the slippage (his internal resistance) that retarded the redecision work in his head, he challenged the subtle resistances to change arriving from outside himself: socially in his home life; institutionally in his economic life; even culturally. Judd's group experience primed him for these new challenges.

When Judd announced to his wife that he didn't have headaches any more, she was outwardly full of joy, but somehow didn't seem to know what to do with herself. She was used to the old Judd with his sulks, nervous aches, and pains. Her favorite greeting took the form of, "How are you feeling today?" and his typical response was, "Not so good." When he overcame his script injunction, his answer became, "Oh, I feel fine." This was met by a sickening smile from his wife, and she would plead, "Are you sure?" The first few times this happened, Judd replied to her, "Well, now that you mention it, I think I do have a little ache in my neck." Temporarily he succumbed to this volley of *social resistances* from his wife. But he increased his awareness of these day-by-day hindrances in the group through discussion, and gathered support from those who had no vested interest in his being sick (the group members). He persisted and did not bite on the invitation his wife gave him to be sick. Instead, he insisted on being treated as a healthy person, and his wife, becoming more frantic at this point, would say, "It's about time to go to the doctor and get your prescription refilled." Judd's response was, "I don't need medicine any more."

The exchange became more intense, with his wife angrily replying, "Now, instead of pain pills, it looks like you need tranquilizers because you're getting crazy." Escalation such as this is designed to get things back in their old order, and is known as the "second volley" of social resistance. This is a strong test for a person experiencing something new—but it becomes less potent when one is expecting it. It can be predicted in advance that close social contacts will resist the change at least as hard as the person who is undergoing it. The "third degree volley," though, could be the *coup de grâce.* In it, the spouse may threaten to leave, claiming basic incompatibility because she has been robbed of the way she gave and got strokes, and might say, "You're not the man I once married," which of course is accurate.° Judd, at the point of the third volley, had the option of breaking down and going back to his old "comfortable" patterns. But in persisting, he finally got through. A little patience on his part was judicious as his wife was also a flexible human being and could grow in a positive direction.[8] Sometimes, however, an appropriate solution may be to dissolve a marriage and seek out a more complementary partner. In this way, divorce becomes a creative choice which allows for the growth of both parters (or ex-parters). Relationships with spouses, children and other close, intimate contacts including bosses or employees may also be affected, and the individual needs to decide whether or not to take the risk. Many do.

Institutional resistances also sneak up on the individual and usually involve economics. In Judd's case, the vast and lucrative drug industry was involved. Billions of dollars are made every year by the selling of huge quantities of pills. A few of these are life-saving, and some contribute greatly to an individual's health and longevity; however, a frighteningly large number of drugs are not in this category. These are the many, many medicines that have only minimal pharmaceutical benefits and really are, at best, symptom-relievers, and at worst, habituating medicines that have little chance of helping an individual. In my own practice I find that for every prescription I write, nine people are taken off drugs.

When esthenic Judd walked into the doctor's office, he was walking into an institution which like his wife did not give up easily. After multiple complaints, the frustrated doctor, hoping to do something beneficial, would reach for a prescription pad and give him one of the newer pills that had been advertised rather heavily in the medical journals. If the doctor said to Judd, "Look, you don't need pills; you need to get to the bottom of this," Judd would find some reason to abandon that

---

°This is why it is only fair to ask a person in psychotherapy to let one's spouse know that things like this may happen. I encourage the spouse to consider a growth experience like a treatment group for him or herself.

doctor, who was not going along with the pill-passing institution, and seek out another one.° Everything from the manufac-
turer to the Madison Avenue advertisements to the doctor's
office and the pharmacist's friendly conversation may act as an
insitutional reinforcement for the person to stay the way he/she
is. Judd made a joke one time about one of the capsules that he
was taking, saying, "You mean I have to give up this red, yellow, and green multicolored capsule? What do I get in return?
Running a mile at six in the morning!" When he made that
remark, it was clear that he had pretty much recognized the
institutional resistances.[9]

Cultural resistances to personal change are subtle, ever-pre-
sent, and strongly influential. One of our "collective truths" is
that if you are feeling bad, the remedy is to open up your
mouth and put in some magic elixir. Watch television for a few
hours and see how prevalent this cultural scripting is; a woman
will appear with furrowed brow and a painful headache—into
her mouth goes a fast-acting remedy—and presto! She smiles,
cured! The children get a pretty good dose of this themselves
on TV programs for youngsters as they watch little boys and
girls smile with delight when they eat just the right breakfast
crunchies—even dogs are cured of the doldrums as they frisk-
ily partake of a "tasty little treat." Judd remembered Popeye
opening his magic can of spinach just in time to avoid doom
and turn the table on his arch rival, Bluto.

Fairy tales passed on from generation to generation reinforce
the belief in the power of magic potions to influence life. Just
as Ponce de Leon wandered in search of the fountain of youth,
Judd too set about in quest of the elixir for everlasting health
and vigor. All the way back to Dionysius' discovery of the vine,
we have support for gaining bliss by putting something in our
mouths. (No wonder we have a substantial drug culture.)
Judd's mother also swallowed this mythology, as evidenced by

°If patients look long enough, they can always find some doctor to give them
whatever pills they really want. Doctors are hardly ever malicious or out to
make money from overprescribing; rather, they are unwitting accessories to the
health game and believe that they are "helping." However, many conscien-
tious psychologically aware physicians and pharmacists don't go along with
overprescribing.

her intriguing medicine cabinet. These commonly shared myths made it easy and culturally acceptable for Judd to avoid facing his real problems.

The confrontation of cultural influences which prevent change is difficult because of its diversity. Here education seems to hold the greatest promise. Many socially active movements have attacked these deep, subtle roots of conformity; Judd profited by an enlightened examination of cultural forces acting on him, and was able to find humor in some previously unrecognized negative influences.

Judd's egogram, constructed after more than a year of rigorous attention to change—via diagnoses of weak areas, surfacing inner conflicts, confronting slippage, redeciding, practicing, exercising both psychologically and physically, and overcoming resistances—looked like this (Figure F-4):

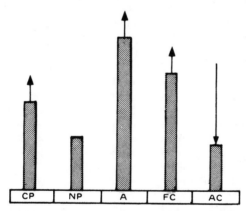

Figure F-4. Judd's "After" Egogram (Compare to his "Before" egogram, p. 82)

His Critical Parent gained power as he was able to say "No" to outside influences and was no longer a social patsy. His Adult gained, particularly in his ability to see himself more accurately; he laughed more, as his Free Child grew, and, dramatically, his adapted Child decreased as he lived out his life in personal strength and freedom from psychological slavery.

FOOTNOTES FOR PHILOSOPHERS

1. The techniques described in this chapter follow a distinct line of psychological treatment which brings inner conflicts and feelings out into the open. I was first introduced to this by Dr. Jacob Moreno, the creator of psychodrama, which was developed in Vienna in the 1920s as an alternative to Freud's methods. A recent succinct presentation of psychodrama by J. Moreno is in H. Kaplan and B. Sadock (eds.), *Comprehensive Group Psychotherapy,* Baltimore: 1971, Chapter IX, Williams & Wilkins, pp. 460–500.

   Fritz Perls, the Gestalt master, dramatically showed how to bring inner, conflicting elements out into the open. He was particularly adept in applying this in dream work—see his *Gestalt Therapy Verbatim,* Lafayette, Calif.: Real People Press, 1969. Of course, the ideas of Eric Berne and his studies on intuition showed that inner conflicts can be seen in the here-and-now as egostates—"Intuition V, The Ego Image," *Psychiat. Quart.,* vol., 31, no. 611, 1957. More recently, Robert and Mary Goulding, founders of the Western Institute for Group and Family Therapy in Watsonville, California, have applied the techniques of both Gestalt and Transactional Analysis in a process through which they utilize a technique called "redecision".

   The processes described in this chapter, which are my own developments, draw heavily from the techniques of those named above, in addition to others.

2. This memory represents many earlier such happenings and corresponds with the hyperesthetic memory experience Freud and Bruerer discussed in "On the Psychical Mechanism as the Hysterical Phenomenon," in *Standard Edition of The Complete Psychological Works of Sigmund Freud, Vol. III,* ed. J. Strachey, London: Hogarth Press, 1962.

3. One aim of TA is to bring the client to a point where crystallizing statements—from the Adult of the therapist to the Adult of the client—are effective. For those interested in the technical aspects of group psychotherapy, Berne's discussion of basic techniques is excellent: *Principles of Group Treatment,* Chapter 11, pp. 233–258.

4. While inner thoughts and feelings become confused and jumbled together, the techniques of separation are enhanced by an actual physical shift when different parts are reenacted.

5. In a weekend teaching marathon group, a lady did overcome a block in a single session and reported to me later that it was a lasting change, so it does happen rarely. She herself was primed for this after many months of work with another TA colleague.

6. Freud relied heavily upon his theory of the unconscious, stating: ". . . the whole of psychoanalytic theory is in fact built up on the perception of the resistance observed by the patient when we try to make him conscious of his unconscious." S. Freud, *New Introductory Lectures in Psychoanalysis,* translated by W. J. H. Sprott, New York: W. W. Norton, 1933. Transactional Analysis is not formally concerned with the "unconscious," but focuses on the dynamic factors in the personality that are surfaced in the here-and-now, being more closely allied to Fritz Perls's notion of impasses. By the use of the technique of confrontation, the Gestalt therapist tries to get to the impasse, which is that point where "you believe you have no chance of survival because you don't find the means in yourself. We find the place where the person is stuck and we come to the surprising discovery that this impasse is mostly a matter of fantasy. It doesn't exist in reality. A person only believes that he has not his resources at his disposal"—Fritz Perls, *Gestalt Therapy Verbatim* (compiled and edited by J. Stevens), Lafayette, Calif.: Real People Press, 1969, p. 39. The major difference between Perls's idea of impasse and that which is utilized in the double chair technique in my own method is that the impasse is not a fantasy, it is a reality; the agent or the force of this comes from the specific functional egostate, which is the most overworked and therefore has the greatest reservoir of power. My method is one of surfacing, so that a person will be able to face the impasse effectively. Perls does rather succinctly state that people do not want to get through the impasse that would grant them development, but prefer to maintain the status quo. He says, "Very few people go into therapy to be cured, but rather to improve their neurosis." (Berne mentions on several occasions that people go into therapy to be able to play their games better.) Dr. Robert Goulding, one of the early leaders in TA who is equally adept in Gestalt techniques, having been associated with both Berne and Perls, posed an interesting structural definition of impasses and one which is clearer than that posed by Perls. In an article entitled "Thinking and Feeling in Transactional Analysis: Three Impasses," *Voices,* vol. 10, no. 1, Spring 1974, pp. 11–13,

Goulding pointed out that there are essentially three impasses—two of which are looked at in a structural matrix. What he calls "first degree impasse" is a message from the Parent egostate of the biological parent (called "counter injunction"), which is heard in statements such as "Work hard." The second degree impasse, also a structural and transactional impasse, comes from the Child egostate of the parent to the Child egostate of the client, such as "Don't exist." This is what Claude Steiner (*Scripts People Live*) calls an "injunction." His third definition of impasse is within the individual, more closely approaching the functional uses that I have arrived at with the principles of slippage. In his viewpoint, it is between the Adapted Child and the Free Child in the patient's own head.

7. Physical anthropologists theorize that the human brain enlarged in order to keep up with new actions—see, e.g., J. S. Bruener, "The Course of Cognitive Growth," *The American Psychologist*, vol. 24, January 1964, p. 15. Do things first, and growth (psychologically) follows. This has parallels with anatomical development, as is seen in the evolution of the size of the human brain. It appears that actions came first in developing more and more techniques evolutionarily, and then the brain grew to accommodate the new actions, tools, etc., that were developed. Therefore, action probably preceded fully developed structure.

8. One of the more dramatic social resistances was seen in a couple who had contracted with the therapist to overcome their sexual inhibitions with each other. An hour before their first session was to begin, they got into a huge fight, the wife received a black eye, and as the therapist opened the door into his waiting room, he met the husband with clenched fists saying, "She deserved it!" and the wife saying, "Look what he did to me!" In this case, the internal resistance (his fear of sex) and the social resistance (her need to be in command, here, sexually) were combined in a dramatic fashion.

9. This problem was discussed on a panel at the American Psychiatric Association's 125th Annual Meeting in Dallas, May 1972, entitled "Pills vs. People," soon to be published in monograph form. Medical journals are supported by multicolored advertisements of poor patients in distress—relieved by the latest drug company offering. Even the Journal of the American Psychiatric Association is heavily dosed with these ads, which must get results as the ads are very expensive.

6

Here's How—Actual Techniques for Personality Growth

There are delightfully simple and appealing ways to strengthen deficient personality parts. However, various resistances need to be overcome; for instance, pounding a pillow and expressing hidden anger may be a difficult task for those who have never done it, although they may agree (intellectually) that it might be useful. Different people have different areas of weakness: some may have difficulty in expressing such emotions as anger, sorrow, or happiness; others may have trouble in receiving strokes or nurturing. There are those who avoid thinking and feel that the intellect is for college professors, while others reject fun and frivolity; finally, there are those who avoid compromise and those who always compromise.

People can easily and freely exercise those parts they already have in abundance, even though the habitual repetition of well-exercised strengths may be detrimental to their personalities.[1] The most effective action is to bolster up weak personality parts:

1. Successful action leads to change, which is defined as *a shift in energy balance in egostates.*
2. Basic techniques to raise the different egostates will be presented, and the advantages and disadvantages of so doing will be discussed.

3. The most frequent resistances to change will be noted, and appropriate cautions to be heeded with any of these actions mentioned.

It is much easier to *raise* a low egostate than to *lower* an excessively high one. Therefore this chapter will not include techniques for lowering an undesirably high egostate. These states will get lower automatically when the desired states are exercised. However, *resistance occurs at this point: when a person works at raising a specific egostate, the higher egostates will engage in a severe struggle to keep their strong status and prevent themselves from being dethroned.* These powerful egostates keep the egogram and the personality "stuck" and work at preventing them from changing. One may observe these battles in action between the strong egostates and the fledgling ones when reading the sections about the techniques used to raise egostates.

THE FREE CHILD

Advantages: Many people want to raise their Free Child in order to increase their creativity and spontaneity. People with highly developed Free Child egostates are insightful, aware, fun-loving, and intuitive. They are frequently lively and humorous. Human beings are born with a natural curiosity and an exploratory nature which may unfortunately be squelched along the way. One gratifying effect of having a high Free Child is a robust sex life.[2]

Disadvantages: An overabundance of the Free Child may dominate one's Adult decision-making processes and may also overwhelm one's Parental values, morals, and judgments. Someone with an excessively high Free Child frequently needs another person to take care of his/her everyday needs. A person acting exclusively with the Free Child egostate may appear to be crazy—schizophrenia occurs when the Parent and Adult egostates are contaminated with the Child. Numerous references have been made about the fine edge between genius and insanity.[3]

Techniques for Raising the Free Child

1. *Belly-Button Watching (Navel Analysis):* A person looks at others around him and wonders what their belly buttons are like. Simply imagining this frequently allows one to smile, titter, or occasionally laugh outright. Many "tough" people may persist in finding no humor in this, so they are encouraged to look around and figure out which people have "innies" for belly buttons and which have "outies." This advanced belly-button analysis usually softens up the hardcore holdouts who don't want to experience their Free Child egostates.

Free Child raising techniques are best practiced in the protective setting of a psychotherapy group or in a social group where people are interested in each other's well-being. A navel analyzer often wears a smile or has a twinkle in her eyes. One tends to be open and receptive when in the Child egostate— often, when two people in this egostate luckily meet, they quickly become friends.

2. *Underwear Analysis:* A former patient remarked that she overcame being an habitual wallflower at parties by going to a social gathering without her underwear. Her secret stimulated her so that her entire personality radiated. She forgot about being self-conscious, and smiled and joked with everyone. An earlier exercise in her therapy group involved the group members looking around at one another and fantasizing about what each other's underwear looked like. Diverse items such as boxer shorts, bikini panties, girdles, and jockey shorts (some with holes), were laughingly suggested.

3. *Animal Farm:* An effective turn-on is imagining the types of animals that other people resemble. Teddy bears, gazelles, raccoons, hippopotami, and woodpeckers are rather common; so are snakes, owls, and lizards. Another jovial experience involves imagining what types of dogs other people resemble. Animal farm exercises stimulate peoples' imaginations and spontaneity.*

---

*James Thurber's "Talking Dog" from the *New Yorker Magazine* and the series of pictures of the poker-playing dogs are products of active imaginations. The Hindu deity named Ganesh has an elephant head and a plump boy's

4. *Nudity:* This is considered advanced underwear analysis. Imagining other people in the nude is a classical technique for raising one's Free Child.

5. *Head Tilting:* When a person tilts his head seven degrees or more sideways in either direction, situations are viewed in a different way. This angle often throws a new light on situations, as has been scientifically explored.[4]

6. *Free Association:* Saying anything that pops into one's mind with one or more people may have a freeing effect. (This is usually strongly avoided even by those who are in protective psychotherapy groups.)

7. *Childhood Songs:* Singing spirited nursery rhymes and early favorites is effective in rekindling the Child egostate—a form of good-natured "freshman" harassment. It is also used with rookies on football teams to increase *esprit de corps.*

8. *Mystical Experience:* The quest of mystical experiences such as Tarot card reading, ESP, and astrological curiosity tends to raise the Free Child. Successful meditation actually shifts brain wave patterns.

9. *Miscellaneous:* An easily practiced experiment for a person alone is to stroll down the sidewalk, trying to gain eye contact and elicit smiles from everyone you see. Instant rewards and mellow feelings are a direct consequence, and this has become an enjoyable way of making friends for many group members.

Everyone can come up with their own unique techniques, Hundreds have been formally recorded in various therapy groups, and many more thousands practiced. Formulating new techniques is *in itself* a way to raise the Free Child.

Gerson had a tremendous fear of authority figures, and related this to the fear of his father. He felt like a scared little boy with his boss; therefore, he was underpaid and underpraised. He was terrified about asking for a raise. In the therapy group, he shied away from the Child-freeing techniques, although he admitted that his Free Child needed to be developed. He fi-

---

body; he is especially favored by Indian children. Many Indian deities take on animal forms and are praised in this capacity. Anthropomorphizing is a time-honored creative activity.

nally tried a few of the Child-freeing techniques in the group and gained new confidence in his creative abilities. He made an appointment with his boss and on entering the office, Gerson imagined the cigar-smoking boss as a fat little boy in short pants, sucking on a lollipop. Gerson chuckled to himself and promptly asked his boss for a raise. As he left, with his salary doubled, his boss even queried why he hadn't asked sooner.

Resistances: Higher egostates work at keeping lower egostates low. For instance, Gerson's high Adapted Child did not want him to experiment with Free Child raising activities. His Adapted Child preferred that he remain scared and intimidated. Gerson persevered and spent his time doing Free Child activities. He demonstrated that the easiest way to get around an egostate that's too high is to exercise a lower egostate. By thinking about lollipops, you are no longer scared or worried about a boss's anger. Resisting change (or overly high egostates) occurs in many ways. An encounter group leader said suddenly, "Let's all take off our clothes!" There was a wide array of responses. An indignant matron huffed, "How dare you!" (high Critical Parent). Another responded with, "Oh, no! Hee-hee, I'm too fat" (high Adapted Child). A third looked at the leader seriously and thought, "I wonder what he means by that—this is an interesting experiment" (high Adult). Two people tittered and quickly tossed off their shoes (high Free Child). One woman chided the leader gently with, "Do you think it will be helpful for everyone?" (high Nurturing Parent). This simple experiment revealed an important finding about resistances. A person's highest egostate will characteristically take charge during a moment of stress. This egostate will take command in order to *resist* change and preserve the status quo. (You can get clues as to your own highest egostate by focusing on the feelings that you generated while reading the list of Free Child raising techniques.) The strongest and most verbal resistances usually come from the Critical Parent. A Critical Parent emphasizes that people should be more serious and hardworking. The person with a high Critical Parent often answers that he is being an Adult, but the phrases "You need" or "You should" quickly indicate the underlying egostate.

The Nurturing Parent seldom interferes with the Free Child.

However, an overly strong or troublesome Nurturing Parent will say, "That was fun, but what about your deeper feelings?" These sorts of statements can smother the growth of the Free Child.

The Adult is a common culprit in preventing the development of the Free Child in that it may inhibit with such questions as, "Do you have a controlled statistical research study on laughter?"

A high Adapted Child may assume a pained expression and moan, "I can't think of anything to do that is Free Child. My mind is a blank." A common Adapted Child vocabulary consists of "should" and "supposed to."

Caution: Don't use an overabundance of Free Child in the presence of a powerful personal authority figure (such as your boss) if he/she dislikes fun and can fire you. In these instances, one's Free Child needs to consult one's Adult to determine whether it's a safe time and place to play. Using the same Free Child exercises over and over again becomes boring, cute, or gimmicky. This is known as third-grade humor. Continual discovery of new techniques is more fruitful than polishing up the old ones.

THE ADULT

Advantages: A functioning Adult egostate thinks well in difficult situations and handles the details of everyday routines. The Adult balances the checkbook, crosses a busy street, and is a frequent consultant to the other egostates. When the Adult and Free Child work together, creativity results. Because the Adult is non-emotional, it is an effective state to use in dealing with problems.

Disadvantages: When too much energy is concentrated into Adult thinking, one may expect to have a boring social life. An accountant with high Adult will not make a big hit at a singles cocktail party by discussing the totals and sums on his ledgers for that day. Also, people who show few facial expressions are frequently avoided.

Techniques for Raising the Adult

1. *Scientific Thinking:* This type of thinking embodies the quartet of *observation, hypothesis, experimentation,* and *conclusion.* Every category provides both immediate and long-range ways of strengthening one's Adult. A pertinent case history will be provided to illustrate each.

(a) Observation: A group therapy member named Willy frequently felt confused so he decided to raise his Adult. He was encouraged to make observations about what was happening between others in the group. Willy pretended to be a Martian from outer space: he began to take notes and describe the events that took place within the group. During one meeting, Willy reported that Helen apologized to Joe with a sneer on her face while Joe sarcastically reported that it was all right. These exchanges then set up a new fight between Helen and Joe. Willy was congratulated for his scientific, factual observations and the group regarded him with a new respect.

Anybody can strengthen his/her Adult by using the "Martian" position, which means observing what is happening without being emotionally involved. The Martian position is frequently helpful to those who feel bad during conversations with other people without actually knowing why. From the Martian position, one is able to view bodily postures and gestures which many convey subtle, threatening undertones.

Family reunions, such as Thanksgiving dinner, are often emotionally painful experiences. Joan suffered from recurrent depressions and frequently left family celebrations feeling that she was a failure. She was encouraged to use the Martian approach in her group therapy sessions, and decided to use it at her next family gathering. She *observed* the conversation between herself and her mother. She noticed her mother tightening her lips as she asked why Joan was not married, and her eyebrow raised as she quizzed, "Haven't you met any nice young men lately?" By being a Martian, Joan observed her mother's Critical Parent scolding the guilty Adapted Child in herself for not being married. However, her Martian position (Adult) removed her from the victim (guilty Adapted Child) position and enabled her unemotionally to observe what was happening.[5]

(b) Hypothesis: A hypothesis is a tentative guess designed to answer *why* things are happening; a hypothesis answers specific questions and gives a probable estimate of the results. Hypotheses in psychotherapy frequently deal with questions about why people do things to each other. The quest to explain *why* has been a hallmark of many types of psychotherapy.* For those who wish to increase their thinking capabilities, a rational Adult approach in seeking probable hypotheses has been beneficial. However, constant question-asking or "head-tripping" is undesirable, and may be avoided by asking the *why* in the present tense. This eliminates delving into past reasons (archeological) or double-guessing future propositions (fortune telling). When Tipsy asked, "Why did I get drunk last week?" his Adult was interrupted by his Adapted Child, which kept rationalizing and apologizing for his behavior. Had Tipsy said, "Why am I on my way to the bar right now?" his Adult could answer that he was lonely and sad *at this time.* The asking of a here-and-now question is an important Adult exercise because answers, rather than excuses or conjectures, are available.

(c) Experimentation: By experimenting, one may validly test the answer to "How will I know if I am correct in my hypothesis?" Mr. Edgy nervously swung his leg in the group. When he was asked why he was doing this, Mr. Edgy replied that he was nervous about sitting next to Bart. Checking out hypotheses is a simple scientific experiment which exercises the Adult. Simply ask Mr. Edgy to sit somewhere else. If he stops swinging his leg when he moves away from Bart then his hypothesis is correct; if Edgy continues to swing his leg nervously after he changes seats, his hypothesis is incorrect. This process of "checking things out"—experimenting—is of course more complex in most situations, yet practicing it demands Adult involvement.

---

*This is not of course the unique concern of psychotherapists, since religious persons, mystics, astrologers, and others also concern themselves with telling people *why* they behave as they do.

(d) Conclusion: A conclusion is a final statement that supports the description, hypothesis, and experiment. The conclusion that could be reached about Mr. Edgy would be confirmed if his leg-swinging stopped when he shifted seats.

2. *Blackboard (or a Pencil and a Paper):* Writing on a blackboard is a "hooker" to Adult thinking. Since kindergarten, people have learned and passed on diverse information by using a blackboard. Written words and symbols provide a visual aid for the observer, who may then be encouraged to think about possible solutions. Confused people occasionally find relief by writing down their ideas and sorting out their thoughts on paper.

Sparky, a feisty but delusional man, got into a panic and phoned me at 3:00 A.M. exclaiming, "They're shining lights and coming for me!" I instructed Sparky to get a piece of paper and a pencil and draw the three egostate circles that he had drawn on the blackboard in my office the previous week. When told to label them appropriately as the Parent, Adult, and Child, Sparky became angry and unintelligible. I insisted, and also told him to write down the appropriate sentences from each egostate about what was happening. Sparky was told to bring these results to his 9:00 A.M. appointment the following morning. His thinking exercise came out as follows: "My Parent says to be scared and hide because lights are flashing at me. My Adult says that cars are driving past my apartment with their lights on because it is dark outside." Sparky chose to listen to his Adult; instead of being a "crazy" person, he became knowledgeable and felt relieved as he left the office and went to his job.[6] During any stressful moment, it is helpful to compose an Adult paraphrase of the situation.

3. *Formal Learning:* Enrolling in classes and programs designed to increase knowledge is an effective Adult strengthener. This is useful for non-thinking drinkers, who shut out the Adult messages as well as Parent dictates. One heavy drinker's cure was solidified when he enrolled in a college algebra course. Drinking and algebra are like oil and water—they don't mix.

Reading factual data successfully raises the Adult. History

books, language texts, and self-help manuals will work well. Learning technical skills will also stimulate a dormant Adult, as will any kind of data collecting and information sorting.

Resistances: Resistance to raising the Adult frequently comes from the Adapted Child. "I can't possibly think because my mind is a blank," or, "How could you expect me, with my neurosis, to think?" An individual with a high Adapted Child uses numerous excuses to avoid reading, observing, and thinking. The Free Child may squelch Adult thinking by saying, "My creativity will be ruined by taking an algebra class." An over-Nurturing Parent may interfere with Adult thinking, particularly around overeating. Momma says, "Eat this, dear; I made it specially for you." Tubby replies, "Aw, Mom, I'm on a diet and apple pie has too many calories." Momma then says, "Tubby, dear, I love you and my pie is good for you." Nurturing Momma may successfully decommission Tubby's Adult energy. Tubby's own Nurturing Parent may also tell him, "You deserve extra desserts for being so good." In any situation, the Critical Parent may say, "What I'm saying is Adult—damn it!" Which means, "My way is the right way." The Critical Parent may correlate being Adult with being "mature."*

Cautions: Don't confuse the Adult with the Adapted Child. The Adapted Child frequently appears like a bright-eyed little professor when feeling that he/she is supposed to act brilliant. This type of Adapted Child may recite for his/her parents' friends, become known as the "teacher's pet," or be referred to as "Momma's little darling." The Free Child, in contrast, operates with genuine responses and feelings, whether others like it or not; and the Adult delivers logical, rational statements without seeking praise or applause. The Adult remains computer-like in its functioning.

THE NURTURING PARENT

Advantages: The Nurturing Parent provides warmth and promotes growth. This loving part of the personality delights

---

*"Mature" is how the Adapted Child behaves in deference to a Parent transaction by doing things the Parent's way. In this context, maturity means: "If you eat, think, and perform my way, I'll call you a mature adult."

in contributing to other people's development. The Nurturing Parent comprises a primary ingredient for a lasting marriage, and it provides an agreeable way of giving and getting strokes. The nurturing that takes place in a game-free environment profoundly influences the attainment of intimacy.

Disadvantages: Overnurturing may smother the recipient and encourage various degrees of dependency, anger, rebellion, and obligation on the part of the receiver. In addition, hard feelings, resentment, and avoidance may occur when the receiver has been given too many strokes, gifts, or services. Overnurturers give away many more strokes than they receive; in order to compensate for this imbalance, they seek substitutes such as overeating, overdrinking, over-pill-taking, and overvisiting the doctor's office.

An overnurturer came into my office and said, "Gee, Doctor, you look tired today. Is there anything I can do for you?" I chuckled and replied, "Wait a minute. I was going to ask what I could do for you!"

Techniques for Increasing the Nurturing Parent

1. *Hugging:* An enthusiastic hug is an immediate, easily learned exercise which will increase the Nurturing Parent. A pat on the back and sympathizing looks are other nurturing gestures. Those people who are raising a low Nurturing Parent are encouraged to focus their interest on others and their problems.

2. *Sensitivity:* Becoming sensitive to unhappy, suffering people and offering guidance and understanding is an immediate way to strengthen the Nurturing Parent. One can be on the alert for those who are feeling remorseful, guilt-ridden, or lonely. Self-nurturing is highly encouraged for those who are hard on themselves. The use of two chairs is an effective procedure for practicing self-nurturing. Tina looked like a sad little girl as she sat in her chair and mourned, "No one loves me. I'm no good, and I'll always be alone." She was told to change into another chair and speak to that little girl with her Nurturing Parent. With some difficulty, she said, "Don't worry, you're a sweet person to be with, you're nice to other people, and you'll

find someone in your life who will appreciate that." When Tina returned back to the other chair, she felt much better because of the reassurance. Other ways to raise the Nurturing Parent are to do volunteer work, or join Big Brothers, Big Sisters, Nurses Aid, and other help-oriented groups.

3. *Giving Positive Strokes:* Giving authentic praise about admirable traits in others is desirable.[7] Of course, game behavior such as "I can't find anything nice to say about her" may be prevalent in the early stages, but this dissipates when genuine nurturing strokes are given. In the beginning, giving out strokes may feel phony; this is one reason why practicing stroke-giving is effective in the supportive setting of a therapy group.

4. *Cooking for Others:* Food preparation is a popular nurturing activity (see Mary's Orgasm, Chapter Two). A high Nurturing Parent often brings people cookies, poems, flowers, and other gifts. But a person who overnurtures may end up with a personal stroke deficit (see Big Mama, Chapter Nine).

Resistances: A person who is raising one's Nurturing Parent may be confronted by his/her Adapted Child, who begins demanding more attention and strokes than the Nurturing Parent is willing to give out. In my TA groups, a person with a high Adapted Child may be full of reasons why other people should talk about "my" problem. In social encounters, the person with a high Adapted Child may appear selfish, but this is often symptomatic of his/her nonacceptance or nonassimilation of positive strokes. Surprisingly, the cure for this type of Adapted Child behavior is to raise the Nurturing Parent toward himself/herself and others. Giving and accepting strokes follows the "tit for tat" finding, as Mary discovered.

The Critical Parent has adept slogans to squelch the Nurturing Parent. "Get them before they get you!", "Don't give anything to people because they won't give it back." Adhering to these mottos prevents effective nurturing. The Free Child may step in and poke fun at someone who is practicing how to nurture, and this may further inhibit him/her. The Adult may interfere by setting up a head trip which involves an intellectual discourse about why, when, and where to nurture.

Cautions: Avoid practicing nurturing techniques with rip-off artists and dependent sorts who appear "needy." Avoid those who continually ask for too much, or if this is not possible, seek out acquaintances who may balance this deficit. Watch for the authentic qualities to be praised in others.

THE CRITICAL PARENT

Advantages: Displaying a healthy amount of Critical Parent protects a person and prevents him/her from being a slave to other people's whims. People with low or almost nonexistent Critical Parent egostates are easily pushed around and taken advantage of. A low Critical Parent neither stands up for his/her rights nor defends his/her opinions. A poignant example of the positive value of the Critical Parent was demonstrated by Rhett Butler in *Gone with the Wind.* His love, Scarlett O'Hara, tormented and tortured him over the years while Rhett remained her patsy. At the end, Scarlett finally in her dilemma said to Rhett, "What am I going to do?" Rhett paused, gave her a hard stare, and answered, "Frankly, my dear, I don't give a damn!" A surge of thunderous applause from the movie audience accompanied Rhett's assertive decision. He ended his quest of trying to make Scarlett happy when she seemingly would never be satisfied. A great advantage of the Critical Parent is that it can take care of itself and say "No!" at the appropriate time. It is very useful when applied in a political or social way against injustice and oppressions that are being committed in society.

Disadvantages: An overly high Critical Parent is usually punitive and prejudiced. A high Critical Parent may be a bully and inhibit others. While some people ignore this type, others fear and obey such a person.

Techniques for Strengthening the Critical Parent

1. *Critical Comments:* Low Critical Parent types are encouraged to build up self-protection by confronting the things in others that they do not like or agree with. Somebody develop-

ing a Critical Parent comes to realize that each person is responsible for taking care of himself/herself. A person can raise his/her self-esteem by saying what he/she really thinks.

2. *Double Chair Technique:* ° A person with a low Critical Parent is asked to fantasize about someone else who they consider to be unfair and play as if that rude person is facing him/her in an empty chair. This fantasized person often turns out to be a boss, a mate, or a parent. The client with a low Critical Parent is then encouraged to direct authentic critical feelings toward the fantasized person. Specific critiques are encouraged. Although this is a relatively simple exercise, it can have far-reaching effects for those who are timid in fighting for themselves and standing up for their rights.

Pat was an apartment manager with a low Critical Parent, who was sandwiched between his landlord and the tenants. (People with low Critical Parents tend to find themselves in jobs like these.) Both sides berated him for doing a lousy job; collecting rents on time for the landlord and keeping up with the repairs for the tenants. Because Pat felt he was unable to make either side happy, the harder he tried to please, the more depressed he became. In his TA group, he first placed his boss in the empty chair and said the things he was unwilling to say previously. Then he seated his imaginary tenants in other chairs and expounded his feelings. A big smile spread over his face when he discovered he could actually express his anger. A few weeks later, he asked if he could place his mother in the empty chair. He became furious at how she had taught him to say only nice things to people.°° After strengthening the critical parts of his personality, he began to practice his self-assertiveness on the outside. The next time his boss nagged him, he countered with a glare and the statement that he was "not going to take any more crap off him." The surprised boss re-

---

°This is only one of the many possible uses of double chair techniques. The two chairs are gradually replacing the couch in the realm of psychotherapy.

°°When practicing critical or aggressive techniques, it is useful to give equal time to expressing positive remarks to the mother.

sponded by giving him a raise (Pat also risked getting fired, which might not have been too tragic).

3. *Pillow Pounding:* Pounding pillows is a physical expression of exercising one's Critical Parent. The person places the object of his wrath on a pillow, then angrily beats away at it. I recommend that some clients actually line up a group of pillows and have a "psychological hit parade." Sometimes a person with a very low Critical Parent will take the pillow home, look at it, then find an acceptable excuse for not hitting it. Support is needed, as resistance to expressing anger runs very high. Permission to do something as simple as pounding a pillow is freely given only when the person is low in Critical Parent. Resistances must be potently confronted—first by the group leader, second by the group members, and finally, by the Adult of the subject. Those with low Critical Parents are encouraged to criticize movies, television, political movements, speeches, and religions, among other things, in order to further develop these strengths. They are urged to vent their resentful feelings publicly. The mechanism of first recognizing disagreeable areas and then actively criticizing them produces the goal of raising a low, ineffectual Critical Parent.

Resistances: The Nurturing Parent may inhibit the fledgling Critical Parent by saying, "Turn the other cheek," "Love thy neighbor," or, "If you can't say anything nice, don't say anything at all." These messages reinforce politeness and compliance as well as inhibiting the person's ability to make valid criticisms and judgments. Usually, with a low Critical Parent on egograms, there is a high Adapted Child which has learned not to stand up to others. This is deleterious because there are certain times when confrontations are productive.

Cautions: Avoid exercising your Critical Parent if you already have enough. A little bit goes a long way. Don't pound the pillow with anger if you're already an angry person to begin with—practice hugging and kissing it instead. Do not unprovokedly attack a menacing person with a higher Critical Parent than yours. It is not wise to walk up to a burly lumber-

jack and say, "I'm not taking any crap from you, buddy."
Exercise your Critical Parent only when it's necessary and useful.

THE ADAPTED CHILD

Advantages: Most people have an overabundance of
Adapted Child already; however, there are some distinct advantages to the Adapted Child. A major quality is its ability to
compromise, to be patient, and to be tolerant of others. Without
these qualities, it's difficult to get along with and live with
others (see Action Annie, Chapter Eight). The Adapted Child
listens to others and frequently goes along with the crowd.

Disadvantages: Having too much Adapted Child means
complying with almost everything even though the dictates
may be crazy or prejudiced. The conformity of the Adapted
Child may be either compliant or pseudo-rebellious. No matter
which, the whole idea is that the Adapted Child is conforming
to a message rather than acting spontaneously. (See Chapter
Three: Arthur and Hugh with Mrs. Clayton). An agreeable
(compliant) conformity is:

MOTHER: "Eat your spinach, dear."
JUNIOR: "Yes, Mother, if you say so."

A disagreeable (pseudo-rebellious) conformity is:

MOTHER: Eat your spinach, dear."
JUNIOR: "No, I won't!"

Neither response is a creative, free reaction. Rather, both have
a Pavlovian air to them: Mother gives a command (or rings the
bell) and a conditioned reply, Yes or No, is given (the dog
salivates), Mother's strokes are obtained.

Techniques for Developing the Adapted Child

1. *Compromise:* This is a beneficial action for a person wishing to strengthen his/her Adapted Child. A low Adapted Child
is instructed to intervene during disagreements and maintain a
middle-of-the-road approach.

2. *Go Along with What Someone Else Wants:* A person with a low Adapted Child may gain the experience of neither making waves nor creating hassles. A low Adapted Child is encouraged to practice being compliant with his/her mate by going along with the mate's choice of a movie, restaurant, or TV program. These activities will enable the person to experience optional behavior. This is helpful for one who has continually controlled things, taken charge, and made decisions without compromising.

3. *Empathetic Awareness:* Empathy is the ability to place oneself in the other person's shoes and experience the same hurts, thrills, joys, embarrassments, and angers that the other person is experiencing. An empathetic person has a great deal of sensitivity for others' needs. Empathetic behavior is generally embodied in the Adapted Child; however, there may be undertones of the Nurturing Parent also. One can become more sensitive to other people's feelings by instigating specific action techniques. In a TA group setting, a person with a low Adapted Child may be encouraged to change seats with another person who is experiencing an emotion (joy, sorrow, guilt, anger, fear) and then the low Adapted Child person plays out the identical emotion and relives what the other person is feeling. Another way to become empathetic is to look for the telltale clues in others' faces and bodies that illustrate their current feelings.

4. *Guilt:* When you feel guilty for having caused another person's misfortune, you become able to experience a greater sensitivity and consideration for others. Authentic guilt in an appropriate situation eliminates the bull-in-a-china-shop approach in which the person plods insensitively over other peoples' emotions. A low Adapted Child person is given permission to both practice and feel guilt when another person's feelings are actually hurt.*

5. *Accepting Affection:* When people are conditioned to be overly strong and independent, they frequently experience dif-

*Authentic guilt is to be distinguished here from "neurotic" guilt. Authentic guilt is feeling bad about hurting others; neurotic guilt comprises a psychological "racket," when people hold onto their guilt in order to continue to feel bad.

ficulty in accepting complimentary strokes from others. They shy away from both verbal and physical contact. These people profit from being encouraged to discuss the aspects they like about themselves and then by acknowledging the strokes that they receive from others. Stroke resisters are given lots of permission to accept strokes.

Resistances: The Critical Parent probably provides the strongest resistance to developing the Adapted Child. Typical Critical Parent putdowns are, "Who needs others?," or, "Be a man and stand up for yourself," or, "Don't compromise with people." Many similar Critical Parent messages are ingrained in people, and they are antithetical to raising the strength of the Adapted Child.

The Nurturing Parent, Adult, and Free Child may each offer subtle resistances to the development of the Adapted Child. The Nurturing Parent seeks other people to help, while the Adapted Child searches for personal strokes and concern. An overly high Adult resists by remaining scientific and computer-like. A high Free Child resists by being clever and exuberant. Often because of his/her enthusiasm, he/she may fail to recognize the hurts and needs of the low Adapted Child. This happens, for example, in the manic-depressive conditions where the person with the high Free Child plays freely and furiously at the expense of the person with the low Adapted Child whose needs have not been met.

Cautions: Do not overdevelop the Adapted Child because this results in both psychological and social dependence upon others. An overly developed Adapted Child can be caught up in unproductive rackets and consequent feelings of guilt and sadness.

SUMMARY

Each person makes decisions in life which determine the relationships of one egostate to another—seen as his or her own personality. But the process of change opens up more options for social satisfaction. The first step in change occurs when a person becomes aware; this informed individual may then decide which way he or she would like to shift. Because one can strengthen deficient egostates more easily than lower excessive ones, the person involved in change may incorporate various techniques from the sample lists given in this chapter. Of course, personally invented techniques are exciting and rewarding. Trying new things feels scary, frivolous, or uncomfortable at first; this is because of the resistances put up by forces from higher egostates. By detoxifying these resistances (Chapter Five), one can proceed with the pleasant prospect of fulfilling one's growth, development, and change. Unlearning old behaviors and acting on new ways of relating to others is a tremendous reward in itself.[8]

FOOTNOTES FOR PHILOSOPHERS

1. Growth and a sense of personal fulfillment can be attained by the three "P's" of change: Permission, Protection, and Potency. Initially, a person needs the *permission* to change; unfortunately, in many social groups the permission is to stay the same. Protection occurs in an environment where one's new psychological "muscles" can be flexed—a *protective* setting where one will not be criticized or laughed at. Finally, one's resistance to attempting new behavior is *potently* confronted by the person, the therapist, and other members of the group. Although these techniques can be practiced alone, they are more successfully performed in the protective, permission-giving setting of a potent therapy group. Eric Berne called these the three "P's" of Transactional Analysis.

2. Of the hundreds of deities in the Hindu pantheon, one of the most frequently worshipped is Lord Krishna—the playful, free, cherubic god who frolics in the fields with the shepherds and milk maids. Krishna is usually depicted playing his flute, and he is often frivolously pursuing pleasures with the young maidens. He is idolized as a perfect man by the young ladies in India, and he offers them hope of relief from their banal struggles in everyday existence. Krishna may be viewed as operating primarily from his Free Child, although his other egostates are apparent also. He is delightfully depicted in Indian art in H. Zimmer, *The Art of Indian Asia,* ed. J. Campbell, Princeton, N.J.: Bollingen Series XXXIX, Princeton University Press, 1955.

3. See *Differential Psychology*. Anastasia's work is a study of genius. Many childlike qualities are found in both genius and insanity, but productive geniuses have little mental illness.

4. Dr. Franklin Ernst discusses various head-tilting experiments in his book, *Who's Listening*, Vallejo: Addresso'set, 1973.

5. Theodore Reich discussed this from a psychoanalytic point of view *Listening with the Third Ear*, New York: Farrar, Straus and Company, 1949.

6. In my experience, this has been the most effective brief psychotherapy technique for handling acute psychotic episodes without going to the hospital. (Sending psychotics to hospitals essentially means physically sitting on top of them, optimally with love, but more frequently with large doses of medicine.) Doing psychotherapy work with psychotics has many advantages over hospitalization. Psychotherapy aims at raising their Adults so that straight, uncontaminated communication may take place. This is worth consideration when the alternatives become less appealing: more tranquilizers, more hospitalization, more passive patients, and more frustrated doctors and nurses—J. Dusay, "Response," *TAB*, Vol. 5: 136–137, April 1966.

7. In 1968, I suggested to participants of the San Francisco Transactional Analysis Seminar (composed of Eric Berne, Claude Steiner, Steve Karpman, Mike Breen, and others) that we devote a post-seminar session entirely to exchanging authentic, genuine strokes to each other. We all agreed and began. However, the well-intentioned positive strokes deteriorated into subtle negative strokes after fifteen minutes. For instance, a person complimented me by saying, "I really like your necktie" (an authentic positive stroke), then followed this up with a sneaky negative stroke: "I *finally* found one of your neckties I could like."

8. People may be loosely divided into "feelers" and "thinkers." Feelers are found crying, being angry, pounding pillows, being massaged, and experimenting with their gut-level reactions in weekend encounter groups. By contrast, the "thinkers" are not experiencing their emotions; rather, they spend their hours thinking. They lie on analysts' couches and make hundreds of interpretations about what is happening. Because of this situation, I have invented the "cosmic whistle"—a fantasy device that can be blown at judicious times. When the cosmic whistle is blown, I envision all the thinkers on the couch switching instantly into an

encounter group in order to experience their feelings. At the same moment, the feelers in the encounter groups would switch to analysts' couches and commence thinking. My cosmic whistle would disrupt the tendency that people have to flow habitually in the same direction, thus reinforcing their status quo and resist change.

7

The Flow of Psychological Energy (or the Constancy Hypothesis)*

The most significant observation to be made about Mary's egogram (see Chapter One) is that: *When the energy in one egostate increased, another decreased.* Mary raised her Nurturing Parent by concentrating her time, energies, and concern in this one egostate; and this newly directed energy took away from an egostate where she previously spent her energy. Mary's warm and benevolent way of transacting became living proof of her dramatic personality adjustment. Her Free Child simultaneously increased: she would laugh freely and tell jokes; she made quick and rapid associations, had more fun in life, enjoyed her orgasms, and experienced a lusty sexual behavior generally. The group members remarked that she seldom criticized them or herself. Her bemoaning, demanding Adapted Child part decreased in time and intensity, both in the group and in the privacy of her own apartment. In effect, when she exerted energy in one functional egostate, she spent less energy in another. New ways of transacting subtract from the old.

To illustrate the fluctuations and changes in psychological

*This chapter was originally a lecture for a scientific audience; however, several of my friends with nontechnical backgrounds found it an enlightening exercise in basic algebra and were stimulated to see how this synthesized human psychology with such diverse elements as Hindu deities, Greek gods, and the thyroid gland.

energy, an equation entitled the Constancy Hypothesis was formulated:

$$(P + A + C)\,mm = K$$

Each person's psychological energy is fluidly divided between the different egostates. The $P + A + C$ inside the parentheses symbolizes all of the egostates and their subdivisions: Critical and Nurturing Parent, the Adult, and the Free and Adapted Child. This includes the *total* amount of psychological energy within the person. (If further divisions of functioning egostates become important, they would likewise be placed in these parentheses to illustrate the encapsulated total amount of energy.) The "mm" refers to any nonpsychological factors which may contribute to the positioning of the psychological energy in the egostates. For example, hormonal imbalances, poor nutrition, injuries, or sensory deprivation may become powerful external forces which could determine the position and expenditure of the energy. The "K" represents the *constant* factor which shows, in an algebraic manner, the total amount of psychic energy available to each individual. All of the factors—the intrinsic energy evolved from psychological development *times* extrinsic influences not derived from psychological development—becomes 100 percent of a person's psychological energy. By viewing this equation formula, it can be seen that in order for the "K" to remain constant, the energy fluctuations in the parentheses must be in exact accord with one another. When one energy level in an egostate rises, there must be a corresponding, decreasing shift in another egostate to balance the energy homeostasis. The Constancy Hypothesis is particularly useful when a person is contemplating growth, change, and more fulfilling ways of spending his/her life energy.[1]

PEOPLE FUNCTION AS A TOTAL UNIT

A person's image implies that all the different parts are functioning together, and he/she is thought of in that way. Harry

Jones, for example, is thought of as a totality, not as one liver, one spleen, two testicles, and so on. Only when one part gets out of whack does it cause any particular notice; for instance, "Harry Jones's liver doesn't function very well and his skin looks yellow." Some parts of the individual functioning together as a unit can become noticeable by increased growth. For example, Mark Spitz can swim. His muscle coordination and lungs are so well developed that he can swim faster than any of his friends. In both health and disease certain physical parts may increase or decrease in their function and cause notice. The psychological function likewise forms a composite. Consider Helen Cross. Only when one part gets out of proportion—i.e., "She's a crabby nag"—does it become irritating; and like the physical aspects of the human body, the psychological aspects may also be noticed if a particular quality stands out and is experienced as pleasant—"Henrietta is a good person." The soma and the psyche together form the mosaic.

The fundamental egostate forces recur universally in all cultures, in both current literature and mythology. It is not difficult to surmise the ways that the various egostates are arranged among such characters as Ebenezer Scrooge or Little Red Riding Hood. Ancient mythological characters of Western civilization—such as Europa, Oedipus, and Zeus—serve to illustrate the universal occurrences of the Victim, the Rescuer, and the Persecutor, and their different but corresponding balances of Adapted Child, Nurturing Parent, and Critical Parent. The religions of man also portray characterological roles, using creativity, pleasure, nurturing, punishing, thinking, yielding, and following. Every possible emotional feeling and drive is placed into the cosmic soup pot, from which it is stirred around and ladled into different civilizations throughout time. The eras of passion give way to the eras of obedience.[2] The eras of growth and abundance, and the eras of war, pestilence, and famine—all shift and flow throughout history.

The ancient pantheon deities from the Greco-Roman times have been relegated to mythology and history. When a tourist of today visits Mount Olympus, she might comment, "Isn't it interesting how they believed that Zeus used to sit up there?" Some ancient religions, including Hinduism, have not suffered this type of fate among their millions of believers. The powers reflected by the Hindu deities are extant. A Hindu may, from an Adult standpoint, discuss the qualities and aspects of the principal deities: Brahma, the Creator; Vishnu, the Preserver; and Shiva, the Destroyer. Each may be discussed separately, with its corresponding qualities, and yet in the same breath, one will hear that they are all part of the same unified spirit. The hundreds of deities, frolicking and growling in the different recesses, are all part of the Great One—they comprise the total mosaic of the Spirit. Both the fun-loving flow of the flute-playing Krishna and the horrible powers of goddess Kali, depicted in ancient Hindu art with veins in her teeth and blood gushing from her sacrificial, severed heads, exist.[3] A faithful Hindu may call upon various deities under different circumstances; combined, they represent the parts of the universal force, and are seen as both separate and as One.[4]

In my consulting room these same forces of love, joy, anger, hate, precision, lethargy, depression, and elation continually make their dramatic appearances. They form a vital part of human living. Some passions are discreetly kept "under wraps," while others emerge unabashedly. Within any person resides the whole spectrum of human qualities symbolized throughout world literature, as well as the forces which are contained in the various deities and mythological figures throughout time; these continually recur in our ordinary lives. All such behaviors and emotions reside in each person's appropriate categories of Critical Parent, Nurturing Parent, Adult, Free Child, and Adapted Child. And this complete emotive force of energy is contained within the parentheses in the Constancy Hypothesis.*

MOTHER'S MILK

In addition to the universal life energies and passions which reside in each individual, there are other *exterior* factors which may greatly affect a person's psychological functioning. These exterior factors are not primarily psychological in themselves.

*This is an *a priori* definition of categories (see Chapter 3, p. 52: Are More Categories Useful?).

They are represented by the "mm" part of the equation, and are the variable components which concern the exterior biological and social influences. The "mm" applies to all nonpsychological factors which affect the individual's personality, such as hormone and endocrine imbalance, starvation, bodily injuries and sickness, and severe social deprivation—the most extreme being found in the concentration camp syndrome.[5] Sensory deprivation may also have a devastating effect upon both an individual's physical and psychological functioning. A person with an overactive thyroid will exhibit anxious, fidgety, nervous, and overactive behavior. This specific chemical imbalance frequently gives the observer the impression of that person having a high Free Child. Low thyroid productions have the opposite effect. A person with this condition appears apathetic, lethargic, and weary. A surge of adrenalin may prepare a person to fight or flee. Adrenalin secretions are paramount during stress reactions; the pea-sized pituitary gland located in the brain regulates and oversees all the glands, and occasionally exerts a noticeable influence on psychological behavior.[*]

Externally taken chemical agents—which include alcohol, barbiturates (sleeping pills), amphetamines (pep-up pills), cocaine, marijuana, LSD, heroin, and others—manifest a profound influence on psychological energy. During the first stages of heroin use, for example, there is a tranquilizing effect upon all three egostates, symbolized in the formula by the "mm" part of the equation which raises as the heroin dose increases. As a compensatory measure, the Parent, Adult, and Child simultaneously decrease when they experience the vast tranquilizing effect (Figure G-1):

$$\downarrow \quad \downarrow \quad \downarrow \quad \uparrow$$
$$(P + A + C)\,mm = K$$

Figure G-1. First Stage of Heroin Usage

[*] Almost all of the other glands exert a strong influence on human moods and behavior. Occasionally, tumors give off internal toxins and mask themselves as nervous conditions, which is one reason why a person should first tend to his/her physical health and have a thorough examination if a mood change has recently occurred.

The effect lasts for the amount of time that the ingested heroin permits, which is dependent in turn upon the user's unique tolerance for the drug. When the amount of heroin in the bloodstream decreases, the "mm" likewise goes down. The resulting effect upon the egostates is tremendous. The person's Adult and Child become highly motivated to procure more heroin rapidly—and at any cost. This rapid activity exists until more heroin is obtained so that the tranquil phase may start anew. Heroin effects are analogous to the dynamics of an infant receiving "mother's milk." When it is cut off at an inopportune moment, the infant may experience anxiety and perhaps a fit. One of the greatest pains that an infant can endure is premature or abrupt separation from its mother. The abandoned baby will shriek, wail, and eventually withdraw if it is not promptly reunited. Few things have as deleterious an effect as a severed relationship with Mother. She is the vital ingredient for an infant's security, protection, and welfare. This is partly why sudden withdrawals from heroin, alcohol, and other drug activities are accompanied by a frenzied, childlike activity. When the Child part panics, it overwhelms both the Parent and the Adult parts. A deprived addict may desperately rob or turn to prostitution in order to regain his/her "mm." A mother who torments her infant with abandonment is similar to a heroin peddler who has a sadistic streak.

The greatest travesty is to "burn" the addict by slipping him fake stuff consisting of sugar, water, or starch. The addict's response when he discovers that he got phony stuff is as exasperating as it is to a baby who expected but did not get the mother's nipple.[6]

Other external chemical agents act selectively on the different egostates. Alcohol, a commonly used agent, works like a "window shade" upon the Parent, Adult, and Child (see Figure G-2). The initial consumption begins its effects by gradually blocking out the Parent. It then moves to eliminate the Adult, and ultimately decommissions the Child. Alcohol becomes a progressive egostate depressant rather than a stimulant.

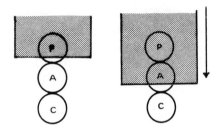

Figure G-2. Window-shade Effect of Alcohol

With a tiny amount of alcohol, certain aspects of the Parent are decommissioned. An individual may act frisky, ribald, and daring, as some of his/her specific Parental inhibitions have been doused. The Adult may remain intact, and will be able to drive the car, obey the street signals and speed limits, and eventually find the way home. With more alcohol, the shade comes down further, and the Adult will be unable to perform adequately. He/she may have to be escorted home and put to bed like a baby. The few who continue to drink after this point may come close to or actually kill themselves as the Child is snuffed out.

$$(\overset{\downarrow}{P} + \overset{\downarrow}{A} + C) \underset{\uparrow}{mm} = K$$

For each increase in alcohol consumption, the "mm" rises correspondingly, while the Parent (P) is the first state to decrease, leaving a proportionately higher amount of Child. The Child apparently is more free and unconcerned because the Parent is temporarily gone. While it appears that the alcohol is a stimulant to the Child, in reality the alcohol has depressed the Parent, and additional alcohol progressively depresses the Adult and the Child as well. (The Parent returns the next morning to become part of the punishing hangover.)

Amphetamines actually raise the Child first and relatively decrease the Parent and the Adult. Each drug may affect the

PAC structure in its own unique way, although there are many similar traits and final results.

Anything that affects the variables of "mm" (drugs, alcohol, sensory deprivation, isolation, torture, starvation, malnutrition, etc.) influences the person's Parent, Adult, and Child functioning. It is important to recognize that at the time when the "mm" (external, nonpsychological) factors are predominantly responsible for a person's difficulties, psychological therapies are not effective. It would be absurd to offer a starving person psychotherapy; it is more useful to offer something to eat. It is equally absurd to counsel an inebriated person *while* he/she is in that state.

THE AMOUNT OF PSYCHIC ENERGY AVAILABLE

On the surface, some individuals appear to have huge reservoirs of psychological energy, while others seem to have minimal amounts and look continually drained. On closer inspection, this apparent energy differential is not caused by a variation in the total amount of psychological energy; rather it is because these persons have shifted their respective energies into egostates which externally appear to be high or low in energy; i.e., a high energy appearance equals a high Free Child; a low energy appearance may mean a high Adapted Child. (During sleep, the normal outward pursuits are held in abeyance while the mystical, magical world of creative and bizarre dreams takes over.[7]) In the manic state of extreme exuberance, a person will flit from place to place doing things in a very rapid, quickfire way. When one interviews a manic person, it becomes obvious that there is not an increase of energy in the egostates, but rather, an *energy imbalance* between the different egostates. In mania, there is very little calculating Adult; instead, there is a Child running around in circles. Occasionally a manic person will be committed to a hospital because he/she has spent the family fortune, bought five or six new cars in thirty minutes, and performed other fantastic feats that only the Child egostate could dream of. The manic phase doesn't go on indefinitely. The following day, week or month, the Parent egostate returns, and frequently a devastating depression will ensue. It is as if the Parent says to the little Child, "You've had your fun, now you're going to pay the price." Some of the most severe depressions, bad feelings, and even suicides have been documented as occurring after these energetic manic flare-ups.

During a depression, it superficially appears that the individual has a miniscule amount of energy coming from any of the egostates because there are moribund symptoms of inhibition, apathy, and pessimism. The speech is labored and slow, the bodily movements are slight and performed with effort, and a person is likely to stare out of the window for hours on end. However, a high amount of energy is actually being expended by the Adapted Child egostate, which is my interpretation of biochemical research findings.[8] The 5-HIAA chemicals (five-hydroxyindoleacetic acid) are a breakdown product of tryptophan metabolism, which is the chemical that is given off when the muscles are active. During periods of lethargy and apathy, extremely high amounts of these chemicals are present (given off in the urine), which shows that a great deal of tension and muscular activity is occurring even though the person *appears* inactive. In a psychological sense, the punishing Critical Parent and the hurt Adapted Child are working overtime together.

Some other body chemicals that have been studied are the adrenal hormones, which raise the blood circulation and prepare the body for feats of strength when one needs to perform beyond usual capabilities; and cortisone, which regulates the internal fluids. Medical students who seemed "cool" before their exams were found to be excreting large amounts of cortisone. When a person appears to be immobile during a retarded depression,* a very high elevation of stress hormones is found in the bloodstream. The more severe the depression, the higher are the levels of cortico-steroids (adrenal gland secretion).

---

*Two types of depression seen in the clinical setting are: retarded depression, in which the patient is lethargic, and agitated depression, in which the patient is actively complaining.

These high levels are seen in depressed persons who mope around as well as in those who are agitated and pace the floor. There is a hidden but definite egostate activity, which does not surprise the experienced clinician. It requires a lot of energy to be depressed. Similar data has been found for other types of psychological illnesses, particularly the psychoses, in which high amounts of internal activity are revealed by biochemical research.

A relatively constant amount of psychic energy is available to all human beings at all times. Overt appearances, such as apathy or excitement, are expressions of different egostate uses of energy, rather than the actual amount of energy available. The hypothesis therefore assumes that: *Any individual has 100 percent of his/her psychic energy in operation (at any one point in time), and apparent rises or falls in energy are more appropriately seen as shifts of energy to different egostates.* In times of an energy imbalance, the cure is to shift energy from one egostate to another more productive egostate.

Even though there is a fixed amount of psychic energy in each person, this in no way limits the amount of growth that any person can achieve. When a person has raised the Child with its creative potential from ten to one hundred times what it was before, this can hardly be seen as limiting.

THE CONSTANCY HYPOTHESIS RESTATED

When one egostate increases in intensity, another or others must decrease in order to compensate. The shift in psychic energy occurs so that the total amount of energy may remain constant. This is a closed system, which has unlimited possibilities. In Mary's case, she became more free and nurturing in the group as well as in her personal life. She shifted her energies from being a critical, exacting, and adaptive person into a pleasant, giving, and creative person.

The amount of time which is spent in any egostate is one determinant of its intensity. If an invisible Martian with a stopwatch were to follow Mary around recording the number of seconds that she spent in any of her egostates, it would find that when it was clicking off the seconds in one egostate it could not be clicking off the seconds in another. When Mary was spending time presenting an Adult dissertation, she was not being intuitive, nurturing, or critical. If one state is actively flowing, the others are not. This is the essence of the Constancy Hypothesis. The principal reason it remains a hypothesis is because the invisible Martian with the stopwatch has not yet come forward.

The Constancy Hypothesis has a profound implication for anyone who desires to change elements of his or her personality. Change occurs when an individual adopts the "growth" model, which means that a special focus is placed on the positive potential for developing weak spots. This is contradictory to the "medical" model, which infers a certain pathology by which a person gets better by getting *rid* of something that is considered to be sick. An individual with a very high Adapted Child, who is miserable and not functioning well, would receive this treatment from a "medical" model practitioner. Remedies, treatments, and medicaments would be employed to chop away the Adapted Child. The "growth" model devotee, in contrast, focuses upon the low egostates.* For example, the Free Child or the Nurturing Parent may be underexerted, and so he/she acts to raise these deficient states. The Constancy Hypothesis serves to explain the popularity of encounter groups, growth centers, and the potpourri of sensitivity training schools which have been popular for nearly a decade. Many such therapies have enhanced peoples' enjoyment and potential. A person may experience relief and a permanent cure from an annoying personality trait by working upon raising a deficient part. If one grows into new horizons, this automatically eliminates the time being spent in old pathology. *The common denominator of change is a shift in psychological energy.*

---

*Being educated in the medical model but enamored of the growth model, I find that the competition between these two schools of thought is unnecessary. A mutual cooperation between both produces the best results.

FOOTNOTES FOR PHILOSOPHERS

1. L. Kubie, "Instincts and Homeostasis," *Psychosomatic Medicine,* vol. 1, no. 15, 1948. Lawrence Kubie challenged the concept of homeostasis as applied to psychic energy; however, he was directing his arguments to the concepts of Freudian psychoanalysts of the day. Cf. W. B. Cannon, *The Wisdom of the Body,* New York: W. W. Norton, 1932, who describes the concept of homeostasis as the self-regulating physiological processes of individual tissues and organisms. Claude Bernard, *Leçons sur les propriétés physiologiques et les altérations pathologiques des liquides de l'organisme.* Paris: Baillière, 1859 (2 vols.), described the internal environment of living cells and the continual efforts of the body to maintain constancy of the bodily fluids, chemical constitution, acid-base balance, and temperature.

2. G. Taylor, *Sex in History,* London and New York: Thames & Hudson, 1954. This presents an interesting view of the pendulum effect of history, which is based upon sexuality in matriarchal (permissive) as contrasted with patriarchal (strict) times. In eras of sexual repression ribald literature flourishes.

3. H. Zimmer, *The Art of Indian Asia.* In plate 424, Kali is pictured as an ugly menacing monstress with bulging eyes, sharp nose, and greedy tongue. Elsewhere she has frequently been depicted holding a severed human head, from which blood is freely spurting into the mouths of female attendants, while other mortals fly about. Commonly she is seen standing upon huge piles of dead corpses. At first look, it is typical to have an ugh-type of response to this primal archaic representation of horror. Kali is commonly cast in bronze statues which have been produced since Hindu antiquity, and is an appropriate depiction of an archaic image. The most complete presentation of all human forces is found in Joseph Campbell's *Mythic Image,* Princeton, N.J.: Princeton University Press, 1974.

4. This unity of opposites is found throughout Indian art but is nowhere better illustrated than on the motif of the sacrificial goblet of King Gudea of Lagash. This finding from the ancient Mesopotamian city of Sumer (2600 B.C.) displays the entwined serpents illustrating the powers of earth facing the fabulous bird representing the sky. (see Figure G-3):

Figure G-3. Mesopotamian Sacrificial Goblet

This motif is still found in southern Indian folk art, and symbolizes the bringing together of the great opposites. See H. Zimmer
(ed. J. Campbell) *Myths and Symbols in Indian Art and Civilization,* Princeton, N.J.: Bollingen Series IV, Princeton University
Press, 1946. The three-headed sculpture of the principal deity
Brahma, the Creator; Vishnu, the Preserver; and Shiva, the Destroyer; are further illustrations of the union of forces into the
One. This is found at the Elephanta Cave, near Bombay, and
dates to approximately the eighth century A.D. See plate 33 in *ibid.*

5. The influence of this had been profoundly discussed by V. Fran-
    kel, *From Death-Camp to Existentialism,* Boston: Beacon Press,
    1959.

6. One night when Eric Berne was discussing heroin addiction
    problems at the San Francisco Seminar many years ago, he made a
    statement about pills vs. people, and quipped that heroin was a
    substitute for mother's milk, hence the "mm" in the equation—
    this became one of the colloquialisms that was popular in the
    early days of the San Francisco Transactional Analysis Seminars.

7. Some sleep researchers have theorized that sleep or dream (REM
    sleep) deprivation is correlated with active psychosis. Dement, W.

C., The effect of dream deprivation. Science 131: 1705, 1960. This means, to me, that when the Free Child state is inhibited during sleep, it may assert itself during the day via hallucinations or delusions. These laboratory findings, however, have been refuted and are controversial. For a review see *Sleep and Dreams,* chap. 23, Kales, A.; Kales, J.; Humphrey, F.; pp. 114–128, in Comprehensive Textbook of Psychiatry/II, Ed. Freedman, A.; Kaplan, H.; and Sadock, B.; Baltimore: Williams and Wilkins, 1975.

8. R. Tissut, "Monomias y Sindromes Maniacodepressionas," *Neurol. Neurocis, Psquist.,* vol. 7, no. 53, 1966.

PART THREE

EGOGRAMS IN ACTION

This section gives specific examples of how both egograms and the principles of shifting psychological energy have proved to be effective for growth and change. After ten years of consultation in both an urban psychiatric practice and in teaching, I have found the four most frequent areas of human concern to be:

1. *Loneliness,* boredom, and withdrawal (see Chapter Eight).
2. *Conflicts in coupling* and choice of partners—whether to stay together or split up (see Chapter Nine).
3. *Symptoms* such as "feeling bad"—which lead to depression, anxiety, or turning against one's own body, i.e., high blood pressure, ulcers, headaches, obesity, etc. (see Chapter Ten).
4. *Authority conflicts:*—an uncompromising individual may strike out against authority figures, organizations, or perhaps society itself. This may be performed either in constructive ways or self-destructively (see Chapter Eleven).

In whatever area the difficulties arise, every facet of an individual's life may be affected—from internal secretions to external social behavior. The *egogram* is a portrait of the personality which is presented and experienced at the immediate "here-and-now" social level. It originated from one's acceptance of early programming by parents as well as from other influences which have now become internalized, as seen in the *script matrix;* and it is reinforced and maintained by the recurrent playing of psychological *games.* Together, these three basic components of Transactional Analysis confront the myriad of human emotional problems. Although these parts may be separated for convenience and clarity, they are all interdependent. See the following case of Jest for an example of how egograms, scripts, and games reflect each other.

8

Loneliness

Loneliness is differentiated from "being alone": the former is experienced as a block to being with other people and is accompanied by a feeling of emptiness; the latter is achieved by choice and is accompanied by a feeling of acceptance. Overwhelming loneliness causes the social skills to deteriorate, smothers a success drive, and is accompanied by desperate and eccentric lifestyles.

A lonely person may successfully camouflage his/her misery. He/she may be continually surrounded by other people and involved in superficial relationships. But the failure to develop intimate, caring, and fulfilling liaisons sets up a vicious cycle that can condemn people to further isolation. The major undeveloped personality areas which cause painful distance and separation from other people are, first, a deficient caring part (the Nurturing Parent); and second, a failure to compromise and accept others (the Adapted Child).

JEST, THE TEASER

This case illustrates the overcoming of loneliness from beginning to end and particularly highlights the fact that a person can be painfully alone even though surrounded by others.

Jest's problem originally came to my attention when he ended up in the psychiatric ward of a general hospital. When first interviewed, he revealed his unhappiness and despair; he confided that he drank heavily while alone. He was an extro-

139

vert and would go out and see people, but few ever visited him as he whiled away many hours drinking alone in his apartment. He was invited to join the ward psychotherapy group and appeared to be bright, aware, and full of fun at the first meeting. He was fascinated with the egogram theory and promptly requested that the group members construct his. The unanimous final product looked like this (Figure H-1):

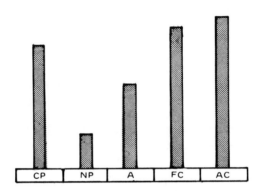

Figure H-1. Jest, The Teaser ("Before" egogram)

Jest agreed that the other group members had accurately perceived him the way he saw himself.

In social action, his current personality radiated an air of self-assurance. Jest was especially delighted with his knack of teasing other peopĺe. His reputation flourished as a practical joker—pranks that were made at the expense of others. Jest had a high Free Child and could intuitively zero in on other people's embarrassing weaknesses, which he would expose and ridicule unmercifully. His underdeveloped Nurturing Paren did not care about their feelings or welfare. People were fascinated with him, but he had no confidants or close friends. At the apex of his loneliness, he turned exclusively to drinking and let his drunken laughter mask his depression. His sexual life consisted of one-night stands, and his work record exhibited an array of temporary jobs. The development of these present-day problems from the past was revealed by his history.

The roots of Jest's lifestyle were germinated in his early family life. Jest revealed how he would relentlessly tease his younger sister at every available opportunity. He liked to make her uncomfortable, and enjoyed her screams and temper tantrums. His father remained a vague memory because he had abandoned the family when Jest was quite young. His "sensitive" mother had her feelings easily hurt and she cried frequently. Jest enjoyed exploiting her because he would then be flooded with attention for his commotion. In high school he preferred "playing the field" but mentioned that he wanted to get married, although he had not found the perfect woman. "Girls have too many problems, and I don't want to listen" represented his basic attitude about women. Whenever a tentative girlfriend mentioned a problem (a normal human occurrence), he would abandon her and move on.

He rarely felt close to his mother although he was occasionally admired by her from a distance. Mother didn't get along with Father too well either, and seemed to be relieved when he walked out. Her own difficulty with "closeness" was finally resolved with her husband's disappearance.

Through her actions and words, Jest's mother praised him for being smart and outgoing; but because of her own early life, she did not offer him personal closeness and did not encourage him to bring friends home. This became the core program by which Jest conducted his later life. His life script is symbolized in this matrix (Figure H-2).

The here-and-now expression of his script showed up in a predictable way. In the hospital group, little Patti specialized

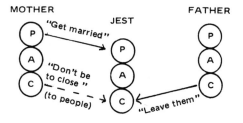

Figure H-2. Jest's Life Script

in being put down and getting her feelings hurt. Her eyes welled up with tears when Jest directed his incisive statements toward her. Patti (a little sister herself) collected many strokes because of her innocent, helpless, little-girl ways. She wore flouncy skirts which she hiked up high when she seated herself. Her major complaint was that men only liked her for her body—never for her brain. When Jest first joined the group, she blinked appealingly at him, and he said flatly, "You're always showing everybody your panties." Patti's poise was shattered, and she began to sob and wail as she flew from the room while Jest smiled. Jest, of course, was correct in diagnosing the pattern in Patti's life. His high Free Child, as noted on his egogram, picked up the subtle transaction, and his well-developed Adult arrived at the incisive interpretation. This ability to perceive quickly and sort things out correctly was one of Jest's strengths; but this demonstrates that being correct is not always the greatest virtue. Some other group members also had accurate perceptions of Patti's style, but they had not confronted her because she had not yet developed a sense of trust, and they knew that merely finding and pointing out a weakness was destructive.

With his low Nurturing Parent, Jest failed to appreciate Patti's nervousness and insecurity. Her sexually flirtatious manner was temporarily important, being the only way she knew of "coming on." When the inevitable confrontation occurred, it would include supportive, optional behaviors instead of exploitation. Jest was not interested in timing, feelings, or compassion, and consequently was viewed by the others as being "insensitive"—but accurate.[1]

He reinforced his basic personality structure as portrayed by his egogram, and likewise followed his life script by playing the "Tease Game" (Figure H-3). This shows how egograms, games, and scripts are interwoven. Jest's high Free Child was active in the "Tease Game" and it pretty well ensured that he would not "be close" to Patti in conformity to his script.

Fauntleroy, another group member, had borne the brunt of Jest's teasing expertise. Fauntleroy was suffering from separation anxieties; for twenty-eight years he had been overly de-

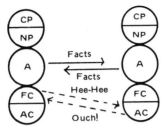

Figure H-3. Jest's "Tease Game"

pendent on his mother. He was now actually threatened with separation because his mother had developed a fatal illness. Fauntleroy literally hung on to a blanket for security and comforted himself by sucking on it. While Fauntleroy was napping, Jest stole his blanket and hid it under a pile of laundry. (Although the others knew that the blanket was symbolic and had to go eventually, they recognized that the time was not yet right.) Fauntleroy panicked, and promptly regressed into the fetal position. Jest taunted him: "The blanket is symbolic of your mother's breast. You're Mommy's little baby! Your mommy wouldn't let you grow up and leave home, and that's why you're here."

Fauntleroy rocked his body helplessly, began hallucinating and banging his head against the wall. That night, a nurse held his hand and consoled him as he cried for his mother's return (Figure H-4).

Fauntleroy was sheltered from everyone by his mother. Whenever he encountered difficulty during life, he would run to his mother for protection, and this showed up in his personality as symbolized by the extremely high Adapted Child in relation to the other parts on his egogram (she fostered this for her own reasons). His mother was quite content to care for him, and eventually smothered him; consequently, he seldom made decisions, as shown by his low and underdeveloped Adult. When his mother became ill, Fauntleroy incorporated his security blanket as the symbol of her; it gave him solace and support when he felt threatened. Jest was accurate in his inter-

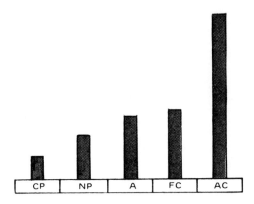

Figure H-4. Fauntleroy's Egogram

pretation, but he was insensitive to the fact that Fauntleroy *needed* his blanket as a Mommy substitute. (Of course, the work with Fauntleroy was aimed at his becoming more secure with himself and thereby not needing the blanket, but this point was still weeks away.)[2]

A vital prerequisite of successful teasing is that it must be accurate, and it must uncover another person's flaw or fear. Jest was exact. When a would-be teaser fails to zero in on another person's sore point, the teasing is ineffective. Teasing is successful only when the respondent panics and lets it take effect. A successful teaser, therefore, has both a high Adult for accuracy, and a higher Free Child for cleverly zeroing in, which intuitively combine to hit the victim's sore spot accurately. A teaser, on the other hand, has a very low Nurturing Parent, and is not sensitive to the other person's feelings. Had Jest kidded Fauntleroy about his shoes, no anxiety would have resulted, because Fauntleroy was not uncomfortable about them. Jest intuitively knew that hiding the blanket—just like teasing Patti about being sexually provocative—would promote spectacular results.

It was not by chance that Patti and Fauntleroy were chosen as targets for Jest's teasing. They displayed their vulnerability with a high Adapted Child, and were ripe to be crushed by a confrontation from someone like Jest who had little of the nurturing aspects that they so desperately needed.

Jest's formal treatment began when he sheepishly confided that his favorite game was "Blemish—Hee-hee," the game by which he attacked other's sore points through humor. (The ordinary game of "Blemish" is similar, but arises from the Critical Parent and has a nagging quality.) Jest knew that it is easy to find something wrong with anyone if you look hard enough. "Blemish" is never played in a healthful, constructive way, because its primary goal is to debase a person, system, or idea. "Blemish" players protest that the blemishes they have found are really there, which is true. What makes them "Blemish" players is their knack and persistence in finding the flaws rather than looking for other traits. Jest prided himself on picking out the peculiar nose, the funny gait, the lisp, and other tell-tale nervous characteristics; in this way he successfully alienated himself from the intimacy he desired.

Jest carefully studied his egogram and casually reflected that if he strengthened his rudimentary Nurturing Parent, he might be able to have closer friends and, perhaps, intimate contacts. This was an elementary prescription he gave himself, which was agreed to by the others. Because this was foreign territory to him, he asked, "How can I do it?" and suggestions were given. One member said, "Look around the room and find somebody who's unhappy. Then say or do something to make him feel better." Jest smiled his agreement and immediately spotted Art, formerly a creative artist, now a withdrawn recluse. Jest said, "Art, I know you've got a lot of secrets, and you don't have to mention that you're hearing voices." Embarrassed, Art looked even more withdrawn and forlorn because he *was* hearing voices. Jest's first attempt at helping someone did not go over well. Jest then looked at the therapist and said, "Did I say something wrong?" Before listening to the answer, he threw up his hands and said, "I just don't have it and that's that." Recognizing that Jest was not committed to change, although he now knew what the problem was, I said, "You sure did blow it. Want to get to the bottom of it?" and he answered, "Yes." So I put an empty "Adult" chair in front of his chair and presented the redecision stimulus. Having seen others do it, he was well prepared to proceed (cf. Chapter Six for the theory of this technique).

JEST (In Adult Chair): "How come you don't want to have friends?"
JEST (Teaser's Chair—unclear what egostate): "I'm better than they are."
JEST (Adult): "Do you really believe that?"
JEST (Teaser): "Not really; I'm scared."
JEST (Adult): "*When* did you *decide* that?"

Jest looked really frightened for a moment, then he said, "I'm scared that if I stay here trying to redecide I'll miss dinner, hee-hee." No one else laughed as Jest attempted to make a joke in order to avoid the redecision work—a predictable resistance from his high Free Child.

THERAPIST: "Your Free Child is working hard to make this funny."
JEST (Adult): "I know it. I'm ready."

After several switches between chairs, he isolated himself in a fantasized bedroom scene with his mother, and then continued:

JEST (Child): "I'm scared. Mommy's getting too close. It will hurt!"

He had a frightened look on his face as he relived an early Oedipal scene and said, "I'm being smothered! I want out!" Silence fell over the room as Jest sobbed, then went on to say, "I'm afraid to get close again."

THERAPIST: "Are you ready to redecide?"
JEST: "OK."

He then proceeded:

JEST (Adult): "Everyone is not like your mother."
JEST (Child): "I know. I'll get close again.

This condensation illustrates how the separation of egostates, and dealing with them in the open, was a strong thrust forward for Jest. He hadn't cured himself, but he was no longer dealing with a mystical or hidden power in his head; the forces were out in the open. He was better prepared to develop optional personality forces. His high Free Child wanted to remain impervious to change, complying with the principles of resistance.* I predicted that Jest would appeal for an immediate release from the hospital to go have some fun and avoid changing. Jest gasped, "How'd you know that? I was just thinking about that!" I replied, "By studying your egogram, you can tell what you are going to do before you do it."[3] This intrigued Jest's curiosity, and he decided to stick with it for a while. He stubbornly persisted in his teasing behavior. Instead of being snubbed, he was given permission, support, and encouragement from other ward members to make people feel good. He relented, and began some awkward practice sessions. Later, he found himself giving comfort and reassurance to the ward members as well as to the staff. He received favorable responses, and began feeling good about himself for his newfound character parts. He jokingly told the group one day, "Maybe I should join the Salvation Army!"

After several weeks, Jest moved into the second stage of growth. Instead of saying, "Oops, I did it again," he would say, "Oops, I *almost* did it again." He successfully caught himself before he lapsed into his habitual, cruel, taunting maneuvers. At stage two he left the hospital, filled with confidence and inspiration, and left his phone number with several of the new friends he now had (see Figure H-5):

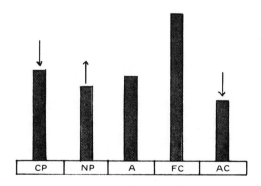

Figure H-5. Jest's "After" Egogram

*Although most people who are sad have too little Free Child, Jest had too much. This again indicates that no one egostate function is "good" or "bad"; rather, balance is of primary importance.

Jest joined another TA group after he left the hospital to further increase his newly exercised nurturing. He was well on the road to the third and final stage of growth, freely doing new behaviors without the necessity of thinking them over first.

ACTION ANNIE

Annie, a college "revolutionary," joined a treatment group with the goal of forming a lasting relationship with a woman. She championed women's civil rights, motivated others to effect change, and was dubbed "Action Annie" because she was a dynamic and powerful woman. Her many strokes of recognition came from political groups, which congratulated her leadership capabilities. Annie lamented, "I've gotten a lot of recognition, but I can't seem to make it with anyone." In her life, she had many companions, both men and women (she finally decided that she preferred the latter). She had experienced many lovers, but her longest-lasting relationship was just twenty-six days with another person. She was intolerant, critical, and impatient (see Figure H-6):

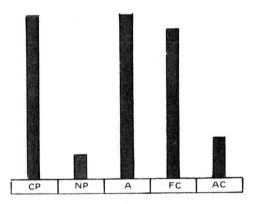

Figure H-6. Action Annie's "Before" Egogram

This egogram evidences why Annie was so successful in bringing about social change. Her high Critical Parent rebuked social injustices; her strong Adult confirmed that social inequities existed; her solid Free Child provided the creative solutions to attaining her goals. She confronted authority figures with a unique flair, yet without conforming to standard rebellion practices (successful revolutionaries usually create their own tactics). She rarely offered warm encouragement to her followers (low Nurturing Parent) and had little trust that things would get better without her intervention. As an activist leader she was successful because she did not compromise; but this was disastrous politically—she was unable to gain a majority vote. The inability to compromise is characteristic of her low Adapted Child.

She was usually found in the Student Union, collecting and transmitting information on campus, political, and worldwide problems. Her usual game of "Now I've Got You, You Son of a Bitch" was directed effectively against the oppressive maneuvers of her opponents. Annie's script matrix (Figure H-7) gives further insight into understanding her egogram.

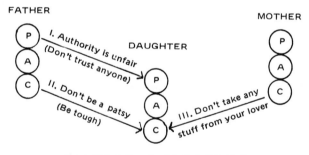

Figure H-7. Action Annie's Script Matrix[4]

Annie's father passed his value system (I) on to her directly by saying: "My boss is a crook," "Politicians are corrupt," and "You can't trust those in power." A hidden but implied injunction (II) was: "Be tough and control others." Annie's mother supplied the "here's how" (III) by demonstrating how to be suspicious and uncooperative with others, including Annie's father.

The script matrix and her egogram clearly demonstrate why Annie had a difficult time developing relationships with others. She was highly successful in dominating and controlling other people, but would not cultivate mutually satisfying relationships. She harbored a nagging dilemma: "If I developed intimate relationships, would my effectiveness as an activist leader be destroyed?" As her therapist, I replied that I did not know the answer. Her desire for closeness prevailed, and Action Annie chose to take the risks. The recognition of potentially incompatible forces operating in her, over which she had ultimate control, laid bare an existential choice.

Annie began by doing compromise exercises in the group setting, which she fought vigorously at first but continued to practice. The main technique consisted of learning whom she could and could not trust; then she focused upon others' positive aspects by experiencing their trustworthy aspects. For example, when May, another group member, said, "I like your new blouse," her quick response was to retort (or silently suspect) "What are you trying to get from me?" Annie was encouraged to "check out" May's (and others') motivations; she found that, many times, people are genuinely sincere in their compliments.

She broke her script injunction by redecision techniques and decided to give others a chance in her life. Her "after" egogram shifted, reflecting an increase in Nurturing Parent and a slight increase in Adapted Child, and a corresponding decrease in Critical Parent. This change did not seem to affect her capability as a leader, except that now her leisure time was spent making love and enjoying her newly acquired goals of intimacy. Effective political leadership is not diminished by intimate personal relationships and compromise (at least it wasn't in this case). This rather dramatic change in her life script served to illustrate that you can change your script and personality without necessarily losing your values and effectiveness.[5]

Annie became more discriminating in the group as well as outside, recognizing that some authorities are fair and some are not. She continued to direct her energies against those who were unfair—but not against those who did not deserve her wrath. With her natural leadership qualities, she was seen to be moving in the direction of becoming an effective political leader, working with different factions, rather than acting as a lone she-wolf radical.

"X," The Misanthrope

A suspicious, distrustful man entered the therapist's office for his prearranged appointment. It was readily seen that he held a sharp disdain for people. Two sessions later, he mentioned that he was using an alias, but would not volunteer his true name. During his third session, he became agitated, explosive, and left in a rage because of some minor thing that was said to him. Mr. "X" never returned. But here is a quick guess about his egogram (Figure H-8):

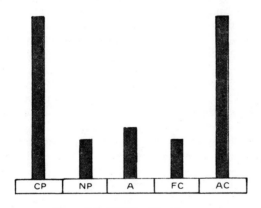

Figure H-8. "X," The Misanthrope

Mr. "X" remained an angry little boy who lashed out in rage rather than dealing with his anxieties. His basic protective position was to retain a haughty, superior attitude toward the "weak" human race, of which the therapist was a representative. His frightened, confused Adapted Child was heavily protected by his powerful Critical Parent. Any possibility of being rational, creative, or caring was completely overshadowed. The

egogram depicts a dangerous miscreant, who could demonstrate irrational violence. "X's" furious and distrustful nature
was unreasonable and illogical (low Adult). Since he would
not incorporate reality testing, a successful course of therapy
did not evolve. Unfortunately, "X's" personality, as seen by his
egogram, prevented him from entering into a meaningful relationship with anyone—even the psychiatrist.

FOOTNOTES FOR PHILOSOPHERS

1. The problem of *timing*—the question of *when* you confront—is
    where the "art" of dealing with others is so important. Karl Men-
    ninger, on the subject of timing interpretation in psychoanalysis,
    said, "This comes intuitively. I know this is a discouraging com-
    ment for students." K. O. Menninger, *The Theory of Psychoana-
    lytic Technique,* New York: Basic Books, 1958, p. 133. One thing
    is certain: the subject must be prepared by developing "optional"
    strengths—and the therapist and environment must be fully pre-
    pared to see their maneuvers through, no matter what direction
    they take.
2. Some psychotherapists tend to reduce their clients to tears as they
    strip away their defense mechanisms by confrontation and the
    demand for immediate results. If the therapist either is not inter-
    ested in protection and nurturing or the timing is not right, the
    client can have severe difficulties. In encounter groups there was
    approximately a 10% casualty rate. (I. Yalom and M. Lieberman,
    "A Study of Encounter Group Casualties," *Arch. Gen. Psychiat.,*
    vol. 25, no. 1, July 1971, pp. 16–30.) Casualty was defined as
    severe psychological disturbance. This, of course, is an extremely
    high rate, resulting in hospitalization, psychosis, or other tragic
    occurrences. Some group members required hospitalization and
    dramatic intervention by mental health professionals. A similar
    rate of difficulty was noted in a series of patients studied in Indi-
    ana (J. Steinberg, "Serious Complications of Sensitivity Train-
    ing," Presentation at the 123rd Annual Meeting of the American
    Psychiatric Association, San Francisco, California, May 15, 1970).
    This is one of the major difficulties of weekend therapies, which
    take on the quality of a hit-and-run phenomenon. The responsible

therapist is one who may utilize severe or strong confrontations, but will do so in a protective setting and will indeed be around the next day or week to pick up the pieces if it doesn't work out correctly. The milieu for confrontation is planned in responsible groups, rather than being random or erratic.

3. See D. Allen and M. Houston, "The Management of Hysterical Acting-Out Patients in a Training Clinic," *Psychiatry,* vol. 22, no. 41, 1959. This article explores the dynamics of an "anticipatory interpretation"—telling someone who is prone to destructive actions what he/she is likely to do in advance. This earlier article was presented in the language of psychoanalysis. Reworked in TA language, it "hooks" the curiosity of the Child, who is intrigued and decides to stay around for more.

4. Berne, Freud, D. H. Lawrence, Shakespeare, and Sophocles all presented the viewpoint that the father has the primary influence in the psychological development of his daughter, while the mother holds the greater sway over her son. Although there are exceptions, the traditional TA script matrix reflects these influences according to the gender of the client by placing Father on the left with the injunction in the case of a daughter, and Mother on the left in the case of a son.

5. The question of whether or not disturbed living affects creative eminence has been discussed by Anastasia, *op. cit.,* p. 138, and H. Ellis, *op. cit.,* p. 138. They found that a better emotional life gave one more creative productivity, so Annie's gamble was rewarding.

9

Conflicts in Coupling

In their relationships with others, people frequently ask themselves, "Is this the right person for me?" Single people worry whether or not they have found their "prince" or "princess"; married people wonder, "Did I make the right choice?" or "Where did we go wrong?" To find an answer, construct an egogram of yourself and your prospective partner or spouse. Invert one on top of the other, and observe the differences and similarities between you. See, for example, Figure I-1.

The overlap in this combination occurs between the Nurturing Parent and the Free Child, and the prospects for this couple look bright. In this overlapping egogram, modeled by Dr. S. Karpman,[1] there are two areas of confluence. The columns are close to each other—they both like to take care of one another (Nurturing Parent) and have fun (Free Child). This couple should last together forever with the type of compatibility shown.

Two people meet at a cocktail lounge and the question arises, "Is this the Prince (or Princess) Charming for me?" Suppose that their respective egograms look like Figure I-2.

The two individuals have only one area of confluence—the Free Child. The probability of their having fun together that night are pretty good; but for a lasting relationship, it would be a difficult struggle. Turning a one-night stand into a lasting romance won't work unless one or both of the partners decide to develop in similar directions. For a harmonious relationship, at least two areas of each partner's egogram must overlap.

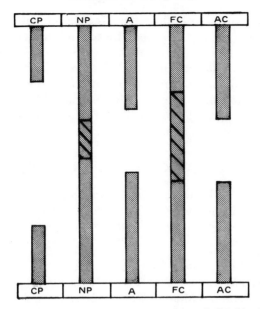

Figure I-1. Man's Egogram/Woman's Egogram in Combination

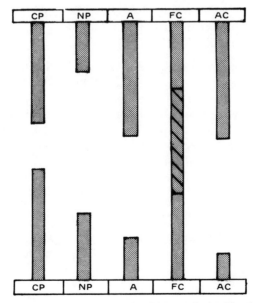

Figure I-2. Prospective Prince and Princess in Combination

These common areas indicate how the couple will spend their time and energy together. When there is a large gap between a couple's egostates, the discrepancy (shown by the gap) indicates game playing and conflict in this area. Thus, two or more areas of confluence promote mutuality. Just one area makes a lasting relationship difficult, possible only by intense game playing; no areas of confluence will mean that a positive, meaningful union is impossible.

TYPES OF RELATIONSHIPS

There are four basic types of relationships between men and women, based on their existential positions. (This applies to any type of relationship, including men/men and women/women).[2]

1. Caveman and Slave Girl
   (Man OK/Woman Not OK)
2. Big Mama and Mama's Boy
   (Woman OK/Man Not OK)
3. Bunny and Claude
   (Man Not OK/Woman Not OK)
4. Liberated Woman and Liberated Man
   (Woman OK/Man OK)

It is important to note that "OK" and "Not OK" are based upon what a person believes about himself/herself and how he/she views other people in relation to himself/herself. Within one of the above positions, couples form their lifelong relationships. For example, suppose a man who believes himself to be "OK" pairs up with a woman viewing herself as "Not OK." They complement each other in a semi-tragic way and their marriage is also semi-tragic.

CAVEMAN AND SLAVE GIRL

Dick was a swashbuckling type who was raised to be quite proud of his penis. He felt that anyone who was born with "inside plumbing" was inferior. Dick frequently reiterated that he was "not going to take any crap off anyone, especially my wife." Dick specifically consulted a marriage counselor after his wife had read a women's liberation article and began having what he thought were "crazy" ideas.

Dick's own mother prided herself on cooking, cleaning, washing, and raising children, but emphasized that Father did the "real" work. His father, a school principal, frequently extolled the virtues of the scientific mind over the artistic. Dick's prominent script message was that men are scientific and logical (OK), while women were silly and scatterbrained (Not OK). Dick's father performed the tasks that really "mattered"—and Dick looked up to and respected him.

Dick's mother encouraged him, telling him that he was an exceptional child. Her looks, gestures, and glances indicated that she accepted the superiority of men and her subservient lot in life. Dick was utterly convinced that he had exceptional qualities. His script developed this way (Figure I-3):

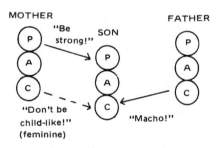

Figure I-3. Dick's Script Matrix

With these early messages and programming, Dick's personality unfolded. In his everyday life, he was overprotective of his frail wife and would caution her about handling things by herself. He became frantic one time when she carried some heavy packages because he was certain it would damage her reproductive system. Here is Dick's "Before" egogram (Figure I-4):

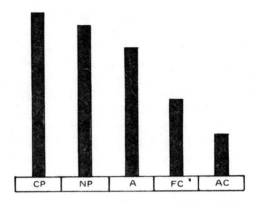

Figure I-4. Dick's "Before" Egogram (Right-handed slant)

Dick has more energy in the Parent side of his egogram than on the Child side. His Critical Parent derived most of its energy from unwarranted prejudices, particularly against women. His Nurturing Parent was founded on the basis that he felt it was his duty to aid distressed, inferior persons. His Adult was exercised through his chemical engineering job.° His Free Child was underdeveloped and infrequently concerned with the quick sexual encounter, because he viewed romance as being feminine. His rare Adapted Child would not involve itself in satisfying his wife or being agreeable to anyone. During moments of anger, he would mutter, "Well, screw you!" He prided himself sexually on being a "fast draw" (the cowboy hero always shoots the quickest).

After knowing him better, a TA summary on Dick revealed that:

1. His usual game was "Now I've Got You, You Son of a Bitch." This is generally the predominant game of those with high Critical Parent.
2. His major pastime was "Microscope," whereby he would extoll others' faults and flaws and derive great satisfaction from doing so.

°All examples have been thoroughly disguised; however, this is representative of his masculine "type" of work.

3. His script position was "I'm OK—You're Not OK." He accepted and believed the program that his family was OK but look out for everybody else, and lived his life accordingly.
4. Dick merrily watched his uncomfortable victims squirm and thereby got his strokes. Occasionally, he would escalate his power by graciously rescuing his victim and be rewarded with a meek thank you.

Dick's wife slumped into the psychiatrist's office appearing dejected and forlorn. When revealing her medical history, Judy displayed a long list of tranquilizers and pills she was taking and discussed the detailed histories of her multiple operations —the holding back of her emotions transmitted into psychosomatic expression. Dick astutely reminded Judy of some hidden blemishes for which she blushingly thanked him. At one point, he put his arm around her and sighed, "How you suffer! Poor gal." Her egogram was the opposite of Dick's (see Figure I-5):

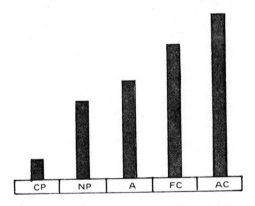

Figure I-5. Judy's "Before" Egogram (Left-handed slant)

Judy's egogram portrayed a left-handed lean which contrasted with Dick's right-handed one. Her Adapted Child was the highest and her Critical Parent the lowest. She shied from confronting or questioning Dick because she felt indebted to him for her happiness, as well as frightened to arouse his wrath. Her Nurturing Parent cared for her family, while her Adult functioned to perform the housework, cook, and get the children off to school. Judy's Free Child rarely enjoyed the brief sexual escapades with her husband and his quick performances, so she preferred to fantasize, read love stories, and watch soap operas. She assumed that she was frigid because of her unfulfilled sexual responses. (Dick was clearly shaken in later sessions when he discovered how passionate she actually was.)

Judy's confused Adapted Child was usually in turmoil because she was engaged in the hopeless prospect of pleasing Dick. Her slavish energies were concentrated upon following her husband's dictates (she took care of him from her Adapted Child, because she was "supposed to," not from an authentic Nurturing Parent). As she was too busy to take care of her own private needs, she relied upon her pill bottle to get her through the day and expressed gratitude to her husband for putting up with her inadequacies, which by this time she believed actually existed. A self-pitying, pouting expression seemed to belie her statement. Girls weren't complimented for being bright in her family when she was growing up; they only received approval for being busy little helpers who were seen and not heard. She had strong parental permissions to be pretty —and strong injunctions not to think.

As a child, Judy felt close to her father, the first important man in her life, especially when she was ailing or ill. He would promptly rescue her by kissing her wounds and chide her for being such a helpless little girl. He chuckled about the frivolities of little girls and sighed about the inadequacies of these creatures when they grew up and became women.

Judy played a game entitled "Criticize Me." Her Adapted Child hooked the Critical Parent aspects of her father, and later her husband. When the drudgery became too much, she would escalate her games by playing "Rescue Me," in which there would be a late-night chase through the city streets to get to the emergency room. This lively action resulted from the union of both her own and her husband's scripts: he rescuing poor, inferior, sick, little her, and then turning her over to a "male" doctor for continued treatment.

Psychological summary (TA language): Her basic life position is "I'm Not OK—You're OK." She received strokes by being criticized or rescued. She became a professional patient, following the script provided by her father, who viewed her as weak and then transferred her to the family doctor, whom she perceived as a rescuer. Later, her husband fit nicely into this script and did essentially the same thing.

In beginning a course of therapy with them, I suggested that they construct each other's egograms. Judy, with her high Adapted Child, said, "OK, but it probably won't do any good." She approached the suggestion from her hopeless, helpless, and downtrodden Adapted Child egostate. Dick, on the other hand, felt just the opposite. He became critical, saying, "This all sounds silly to me, but I'll do it if you insist." After getting into it, his wife's eyes lit up with a bit of hope when she saw that her high Adapted Child was a complementary opposite of his high Critical Parent, and this hooked her curiosity about whether anything could be done.

Dick was forewarned that his powerful Critical Parent would try to terminate treatment early so that he would not have to change anything.[3] Judy chuckled at this accurate prediction while Dick became irritated. Slowly, his Child became intrigued at the psychiatrist's ability to guess what was going to happen. I queried, "How are you going to leave the treatment, anyway?" Dick smiled, "Well, all of a sudden I could run out of money, or I could always buy a new car and not be able to afford therapy." He paused, "Or I could say, 'Thank you,' like I said to all the other doctors who couldn't cure my wife, and just find somebody else." When Dick analyzed these possibilities, he became aware that both his Adult and Free Child were functioning in unison. His Free Child was intrigued with guessing what he would do next, while his Adult reasoned that what he did in the past would probably happen again in the future. He was beginning to exercise his dormant personality traits and this was potentially rewarding for him.

His wife moved quickly and began the task of strengthening her Critical Parent so that she could protect herself. During an interview, Judy admonished me for glancing at my watch rather than paying attention to her. I felt a little defensive at first but had to admit that I admired her newly acquired skill of criticizing authority figures (in this case, me).*

The egogram had allowed Dick to recognize very clearly the overpowering aspects of his Critical Parent; and Judy was able to see how her Critical Parent was so small. During their arguments, they had a new tool and were able to discuss their differences in a logical, Adult way. What Dick and his wife had worked on in the therapist's office spilled over into their lives together. They finally settled on the most enjoyable aspect of change—rediscovering the little boy and little girl inside each of them. This was manifested by a renaissance in their sexual life; they started reading sex manuals and enjoying new techniques. One night they crawled into the back seat of their car, after twenty years of marriage, and made love. The glee with which they told this to me became part of the tangible evidence that things had actually changed. Dick became more agreeable and understanding while his wife experienced new confidence and equality. After some practice, she felt at ease expressing her opinions and asserting herself. Here are their egograms after nine months of exploring new avenues and exercising these discoveries (Figure I-6 and I-7):

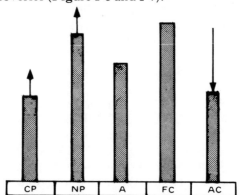

Figure I-6. Judy's "After" Egogram

*Usually, a person who is strengthening an egostate, will attempt to practice first on the one who originally showed him/her how to go about defending him/herself!

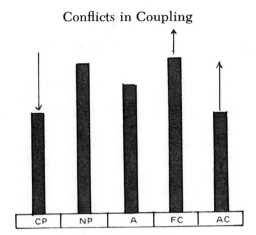

Figure I-7. Dick's "After" Egogram

Dick experienced relief when he discovered that he was not expected to make all the decisions (which was beneficial for his coronary arteries as well as his love life). He acknowledged his wife's independent capabilities, and discovered he had a flair for gourmet cooking—which he had always thought too "sissy" for him. He also discovered that by spending less time in his Parent egostate, his enjoyable childlike hobby of building model airplanes returned. He no longer had the pressure of watching after his wife as if she were a child, and he liberated himself to go and play by himself.

Judy volunteered (indeed, she insisted) to take over some of the responsibility of bill-paying and planning the family finances. Her Free Child was rewarded as she accepted new challenges and responsibilities and discovered that she was quite adept at them.

There were several periods of resistance during the intensive treatment period before these changes occurred, which were handled by the techniques discussed in Chapter Six. Their mutual commitment to the proposition of change and growth reinforced their motivation. By focusing weekly on their personality elements and recognizing how they were thwarting their own development, their treatment proceeded rapidly. Dick and Judy were exuberant over their newly developed skills and complementary personality balance.

BIG MAMA AND MAMA'S BOY

Big Bertha puffed into my office, struggled to remove her coat, sank into the nearest chair, and observed pleasantly, "My goodness, doctor! You must be exhausted after seeing all those patients." I thanked Bertha for her concern, and looked at her inquisitively. She persisted for ten more minutes in this one-sided nurturing, until finally I was able to get her to focus on her own problems. She giggled. "I weigh twice as much as I should." She quickly switched the subject back to her concern for my health. Then she said sheepishly, "You must be tired of hearing about overeating problems."

In the first two minutes of our encounter together, Bertha, had revealed to me her most overwhelming personality component—nurturing. She barely mentioned her own problems and did not ask for my advice. After I ascertained that the origin of her obesity was not a medical problem, I recommended group therapy. During her first group meeting, Bertha's nurturing flourished as she politely dodged direct questions about herself and preferred to soothe others. She carried a large handbag of remedies, including tissues and aspirin; and she hugged and supported the other group members. She was instantly popular; soon, other members gravitated to her for reassurance and support. She frequently brought cookies, gum, and snacks as "nourishment" for deprived psyches. She spent little energy in working on her own "unimportant" problems, preferring to give her time to others. A few group members who played "Do Me Something" attempted to exploit her willingness to give.

Bertha habitually arrived late for the evening meeting. She would apologize breathlessly and mutter an explanation about how she had to rush home from work, feed the family, do the dishes, and then catch the bus. She mentioned that she was supplementing the family's income because her husband had been sick. Bertha's family came first.

The group insisted that she talk about herself during that meeting. She related how the previous day, her husband William had given up his automobile to her so she could spend her day doing anything she wanted. Bertha was thrilled about this

unexpected treat—the first free day she had had off for a year—
and made plans to shop, sight-see, and get her hair done. As
she was leaving, she reflexively asked William, "Is there anything I can get for you?" (She was now in typical territory—she
knew how to structure her time by helping her husband.)

He happily obliged her request by saying, "Well, if you'll
just pick up a little replacement part for my camera, I would
really appreciate it." He was also on familiar ground at this
point.

She slipped the broken camera piece into her purse, smiled,
and set off for her errand and her day of leisure. The replacement piece was not to be found in the neighborhood drugstore,
nor in the next five stores that she tried. A helpful shopkeeper
referred her to a specialty camera store, which was also out of
the part. Bertha spent the entire fruitless day searching, and
finally decided toward the end of the evening to put in a special order for the piece. This, incidentally, could have been
accomplished in a few minutes either by her husband or by
herself, yet she persisted in running errands for someone else.
Bertha's structured "wild goose chase" guaranteed that she
would have no time for her personal enjoyment. That evening,
William asked how she enjoyed herself. She replied, "OK" and
casually told him about the camera episode in a jovial way. She
turned it into a joke on herself, then presented her family with
their favorite dessert. Bertha nibbled the usual tiny amount
that her diet allowed, but late that night she sneaked down to
the refrigerator to stuff herself with all the leftovers. This eating pattern happened every night. When her hunger was ap-
peased, she slipped back into bed and slept peacefully until
the next morning. Figure I-8 is the diagram of Big Bertha's lifestyle.

The single faint line from William's Parent to Bertha's Child
is completely overshadowed by the innumerable lines from
Bertha's Parent to William's Child. This is colloquially called
"364 to 1," and it represents the imbalance of stroking between
William and Bertha. William cares for Bertha's needs one day
of the year (by loaning her the car), while Bertha nurtures him
the other 364 days. This gross stroke inequity *felt natural to*

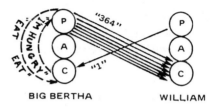

Figure I-8. Big Bertha's Lifestyle

her, as it had become routine and habitual over the years; however, her stroke-starved Child demanded attention from her own Parent, illustrated by the dotted line between her Child and Parent, which is her inner dialogue. Her unfulfilled needs were symbolized by the refrigerator raids, which secretly compensated for her stroke deficit. The Child in her was starved for affection, and later fulfilled by overeating. This game diagram of compulsive eating became colloquially known as "Big Mama."[4] Her egogram was constructed like this (Figure I-9):

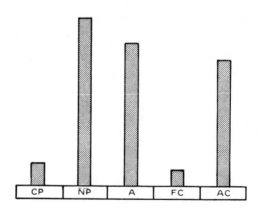

Figure I-9. Big Mama's Egogram

When Bertha was a little girl, she frequently had to nurse her father and make him feel better, as he seemed to be depressed and needed a lot of reassurance. She also babysat, cooked, and did major household chores for her younger siblings. Her background generated and reinforced her unselfish, martyr-like script. It was natural that she would get together with William, a handsome but demanding fellow, with an irresistible little-boy quality. Their mutual attraction culminated in marriage. Soon after, Bertha noticed William's ravenous appetite. William, in turn, would whine when his dinner was late. He demanded fancy breakfasts and varied lunch menus. He was fussy about the care of his clothes, the way his bed was made, and the "sloppy" house. Bertha, with her early childhood programming, would struggle and slave to resolve these problems. When William was resting, Bertha would initiate the pattern by inspecting him closely to determine if he had a fever or wanted a TV channel changed. This served to fan the flames of William's demanding attitude.

Their first baby, William Jr., brought much excitement and joy initially. But William Sr. slipped into a minor depression and was unable to shake a chronic persistent cold. Bertha persevered, and nursed both William Jr. and William Sr. It was at this point that she began noticing a weight gain. By the time her second child was born, she had developed a serious case of obesity. She breast-fed her youngest, changed diapers on both, and made sure that William's meals and needs were handled properly. She had no time to attend to her appearance while she worked harder and harder to keep the family running smoothly. Pounds and inches mounted as Bertha felt that the maternal bliss had turned into habitual drudgery. Diets and weight-loss programs helped only temporarily, as the refrigerator raids resurrected the pounds shed.

Within her therapy group, it was not surprising that she did not ask for a solution for herself. Her conformity to her martyr script was reinforced daily by her marriage and family life. After years of this, it was a well-etched behavior pattern.

The change in Bertha that would accomplish her goal of weight loss could be determined by looking at her egogram. Bertha had very little fun in life and admitted that she was afraid of being free and creative—freedom represented a foreign concept. However, she decided to raise her Free Child and have fun, and also to strengthen her Adult. She understood that more energy in other egostates would take away some of the energy divested in her overworked Nurturing Parent. The group functioned as a reality tester and they would compliment her when she exercised her Free Child and Adult. Occasionally someone in the group would slip and "hook" into her overactive Nurturing Parent. Other group members would confront this once they realized that it was a repeat performance. Bertha accepted the fact that strengthening her Free Child and Adult would entail a strong commitment and hard work. Her entire life was built on a "Big Mama" pattern of all give and no take. She felt that a personality change could have a deleterious effect on her family relationships and decided to explain her goals to her husband. This constituted a risk on her whole life situation.[5] In the here-and-now activity of the group, Bertha was encouraged to be insightful as well as to *demand* strokes and attention for herself. Members quit counting on her for their psychological reassurance. They also began to give her positive support and encouraged her to share her personal difficulties with them.

Bertha now began recounting some of the free and creative years during her childhood. Her thoughts drifted back to her school days, when she would fantasize about having exciting romances and becoming a poet. That evening, she wrote a prescription for herself which included the proposition of enrolling in a local college. William appeared to agree with this, but he wasn't going to let his "mama" Bertha go. Instead, he came up with extra demands and requests. With support from the others, Bertha persisted and experienced a predictable dilemma between feeling anxious and having fun. She knew it was antithetical to her earliest learned principles, and her most common resistance was that school interfered with her family time. This was eventually overcome by concentration and positive support from the group. A part of her continued to feel bad and this mommy part longed to go back to her comfortable overnurturing racket. The support she received from psychotherapy was invaluable, because her family, neighbors, and friends would not have helped her in this endeavor. As her despair and anxieties dissolved, so did her weight.

Bertha became interested in physical activity and found time to walk to school (another self-prescription). She made an interesting analogy in the group: her Nurturing Parent was well developed, like her "muscles of chewing and digestion." Her Free Child was like her underdeveloped flabby biceps. She was naturally more comfortable using the well-exercised part of her anatomy—in her case, hugging others and feeding them. These tried and true patterns felt good to her while her early efforts to attend school felt awkward and uncomfortable. But by the end of the month, it became easier and her Free Child traits of being curious and having fun in school began to feel good to her. She found that the more time she spent in studying and learning, the less time she had for nurturing. Bertha discovered that she was bright; she began getting praise and compliments from her professors and other students. Her dormant personality parts were now in the forefront. She was pleased about her new found skills and expertise in several areas. She even instigated Free Child raising activities in the therapy group such as jungle games (a frivolous activity in which she encouraged everyone to fantasize about one another as wild animals). Occasionally, when she reverted to her uncomfortable feelings in school, she would recall her egogram and undertake a Free Child raising activity in the classroom by imagining classmates and teachers as animals.* Bertha laughingly confessed that the jungle games took her back to the animal cracker days of her youth.

Bertha's evolving cheerful and carefree attitude pressured William to make an appointment with me. His main complaint centered on the fact that Bertha didn't have as much time for him as she used to. William, the other part of the symbiosis, was caught in the conflict of having to structure his own time and satisfy his own needs.[6] When he appeared at my door he looked sick and needy as he presented a long list of his internal and external complaints—the opposite of Bertha's first ten minutes with me. Sadly, he said that he thought he needed intensive, long-term, in-depth psychotherapy (this, of course, would

---

*This was rather creative on her part. Speculating that someone could be cured by viewing others as animals has not yet found its way into scientific literature (see Chapter Six).

take up many, many hours). His egogram, likewise, was nearly the opposite of Bertha's (Figure I-10):

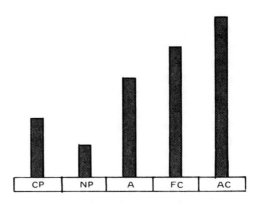

Figure I-10. William (Mama's boy)

William began treatment and described his own mother as a smothering woman who took too much care of him. He frequented doctors' offices accompanied by his mother and began to accept her overprotection. Bertha later reinforced this by helping him, feeding him, dressing him, and caring for him. He confessed that he actually invented new things for her to do for him. William joined a different group from Bertha's. In the first meeting, he made sure that everyone knew his problems and demanded that they focus upon solutions for him (again, the opposite of Bertha). William attempted to set up the therapist to be a potent nurturing force who would give him inspiration, attention, and guidance.[7] After William's egogram was constructed, he immediately decided to lower his Adapted Child on the basis of the information provided.[8] It was explained that concentrating and "trying harder" to lower his Adapted Child would have the converse effect of raising it. To the unaccustomed eye, he would be "making progress"—by which is meant that he would be able to play his game more skillfully and continue to do what he had always done. His Adapted Child would be highly reinforced and strengthened, as he "tried."

William looked like a forlorn three-year-old and sighed, "Then, what can I do?" It was suggested that he pick a deficient egostate which he would like to raise. This could automatically lower his Adapted Child. William decided to raise his Adult, and looked at the therapist for approval. He was positive that he would be pleased, as everyone "should" want to grow up and be an adult. But most people are "supposed to" grow up and be adult. His enthusiasm to raise his Adult was merely an Adapted Child position, and the group didn't buy his explanation of why he wanted to increase his Adult.

At this point, William reluctantly chose to raise his Nurturing Parent and said that he truthfully felt that this was the state he needed to work on. He was given meaningful advice on how to recognize those who needed advice and inspiration. These were difficult times for William, who wanted to be pitied and given strokes from others rather than to give them himself. He would linger after the group meeting to connive extra strokes from the therapist.* I would interrupt this by saying, "See if you can tell me how tired I am." William would consider this, catch on, and smile.

Following William's redecision work, the months passed as he practiced nurturing and fought off his resistances. At home, he took on some household responsibilities so that Bertha could continue school. He awkwardly prepared dinners and was fairly clumsy at cleaning up, as the "little boy" in him fought for supremacy.

At first, Bertha did not recognize this as a ploy from his Adapted Child to get her to scold him in a motherly way, and habitually flipped into her "normal" mother role. With their attention to their personality parts, however, both William and Bertha *recognized this and were able to chuckle about it* as well as use their Adults. Bertha simply walked out of the kitchen and let the slop pile up (no small achievement on her part), and William finally decided to take care of the mess (no small step on his part, either). His final resistance around nurturing hap-

*A group meeting is never over until the last participant has his/her car in fourth gear.

pened in a disastrous attempt to prepare a surprise gourmet dinner. He scorched the sauce, spilled the flour, and broke some dishes—all the result of believing that he was helpless and more like a little boy than a provider. In exasperation, he asked Bertha, "Wouldn't it be OK if I just took you out to dinner?" Bertha refused, and her group later backed her up.

William even accused his own group of molding him into the type of person he didn't want to be. This was a superior resistance and his final attempt to resist change. The group had a natural tendency to defend itself and come on parental by scolding William for "resisting." Had they succumbed to their paradoxical position, they would have finally reinforced William's Adapted Child. Instead, as the group leader, I brought out two empty chairs and asked William to place his Adult in one and subsequently his Adapted Child in the other in order to "hash" over their predicament. He soon discussed the conflict in his own head. His Adult desired change; his Adapted Child was balking and attempting to pass the responsibility on to the group. Recognizing this, he was in a fine position to redecide. This dialogue ensued:

WILLIAM (Adapted Child): "I want out of here."
WILLIAM (Adult): "How come?"
WILLIAM (Adapted Child): "'Cause they won't let me blame them —I have to grow up."

William then looked at me and said that he caught on. I encouraged him to go further by saying, "Are you willing to resolve this with yourself?" William and the other group members who had experienced this before were accepting and knew what to do; he said he was ready, and went back to the Adult chair.

WILLIAM (Adult): "How long do you want to be baby?"
WILLIAM (Adapted Child): "I'm ready to knock most of it off."
WILLIAM (Adult): "You said 'most of it'—
WILLIAM (Adapted Child): "That's what I mean. I'll get cuddled from time to time by Bertha, but I'm willing to stop always looking for Mama!"

WILLIAM (to group): "I feel terrific!"
GROUP MEMBER: "Great..."

William's resistant force fought a losing battle as he himself (more precisely, the Adult in his head) became committed to change. He continued to practice his nurturing abilities and received genuine strokes from the group members, his children, and Bertha.

His proudest moment came when Bertha received her college degree and gave him a spontaneous kiss of joy. He almost felt fatherly. William and Bertha finally experienced complementary shifts in their egograms. William enjoyed being free and not smothered, and Bertha liked having free time for herself and being praised for her intellectual abilities. Bertha and William's sexual life became pleasurable and particularly rewarding to her as she finally slimmed down and discarded her body-covering muu-muus for a body-revealing dress.

BUNNY AND CLAUDE

Occasionally, miserable people unite and lead either desperate, uneventful, or dramatically tragic lives together.[9] Bunny said to Claude for the last time, "I don't ever want to see you again. You're nothing but a worm and you make me sick." Claude then reached under the car seat, pulled out a revolver, and shot her six times. He dumped her lifeless body onto the front lawn, and drove off, only to be apprehended a few months later. The psychiatrist, reconstructing the story with Claude in the county jail, found him to be a nervous, apprehensive, heavy smoker, who looked younger than his actual age. He showed an absence of remorse or guilt about the murder of Bunny, his wife of five years. His main concern was "What will become of me?"

The interview proceeded in this manner: "I don't know what came over me, but how much can a man take?" When asked what he meant, Claude switched from his anxious, scared, little-boy position into an angry man with a tense jaw, clenched fists, and a red face. He yelled, "That bitch! For five years, she treated me like a punk. I couldn't take it any more." Between clenched teeth, he hissed, "She would tell me how much she needed me, and make love to me, then turn her back—just like flicking off a goddamn light." Claude's striking *switch*, from the nervous "What will happen to me" Child egostate to the angry, Critical Parent, happened instantaneously.

During subsequent meetings, Claude related some ironic parts of his and Bunny's personal history. When Claude caught Bunny in bed with one of her lovers, he turned out to be bigger than Claude and chased Claude from the bedroom. Claude hopped into his car, turned off the lights on the country road, and watched as the ape-man missed the fork in the road and crashed into the ditch. Claude howled with laughter as he re-told this episode. He also derived much pleasure in outsmarting others. He frequently caught Bunny telling lies, and used elaborate detection methods to trap her. It became evident that Claude employed two principal egostates—his fault-finding Critical Parent and his nervous, tricky Adapted Child. There was minimal Adult, Free Child, and Nurturing Parent (Figure I-11):

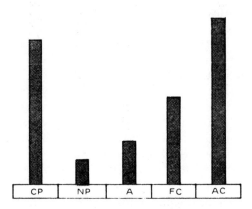

Figure I-11. Claude's Egogram

As a child in his developmental years, Claude was raised by a weak, alcoholic, "wormlike" father, who was continually berated by his mother. Paradoxically, Claude received double messages from his mother, such as "Grow up and be like your father," or, during her angry moments, "You're just like your father." Thus, he was told to be weak (like Father), or, "You are already weak" (like Father). From this, Claude finally concluded that he was weak and ineffectual (Adapted Child): also, he incorporated the critical parts directly from his mother (Critical Parent). She encouraged him to find fault and belittle other people and showed him how. The detective techniques that she employed on Claude's father, such as peeking in the window to see what he was doing, were well learned by Claude, who in turn applied them against Bunny.

Bunny's sketchy history was told by Claude and had some familiar areas in it. However, her father was the tyrant and persecutor while her mother was the weak underdog. Her father often called her mother a bitch and a whore, and her mother promptly responded by being a "bitch and a whore." Bunny's egogram was inferred to be similar to Claude's (Figure I-12):

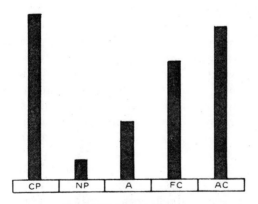

Figure I-12. Bunny's Egogram

Claude told the therapist that Bunny's father frequently reiterated, "You'll come to a no-good end." Indeed, this prediction came true.[10] Both Bunny and Claude continually *proved* that they were "right" when they made their early decisions, which were "I'm not OK, and neither are you." They played dramatic games around their chosen roles. Masculinity to

Claude meant being a worm; feminity to Bunny meant being a whore. Claude condemned Bunny for her sexual promiscuity and she invited him back into her bed, herself *becoming a rescuer.* A dramatic switch would ensue when Claude was frozen out by Bunny, and performed sexually like a "worm," for which Bunny would berate his masculinity. This confirmed his shift to the victim position. They worked at piling up the evidence against each other. The cycle rotated between these three roles, and the ultimate switch in their life drama occurred when Claude pulled the trigger and became the final persecutor—a murderer. Bunny's final role was as a victim. Claude shifted into the victim role when the jury turned the key on him for many years.*

Unfortunately, a change in these types of personality structures seldom occurs; and when it does, it is usually brought about by external circumstances. A dramatic, potent intervention may succeed in overcoming such personality profiles. One effective treatment method has been labeled *reparenting.*[11] In this approach, persons with dangerous and difficult personalities are taken into a therapeutic family home. They remain there for years, and are regressed back into their early childhood days. Then they are re-raised, with both positive Parent and Adult direction. They relearn to structure their lives and grow up all over again. Other types of programs which have had successful results with hardcore personality problems also utilize a strong family approach and esprit de corps.[12]

Bunny and Claude type situations make exciting newspaper headlines as there is a certain mythology about great losers. When actual characters (such as the real Bonnie and Clyde) get together and share a life of crime and violence, they become eulogized as legend. Books, plays, and movies popularize and capitalize on these sensational elements. Starkweather and his girlfriend achieved their notoriety while on a murderous rampage throughout Kansas and Nebraska. The tragedy of the

---

*This is a third degree switch in the tragic script known as harmartic. Banal scripts contain less damaging results but still have the same principal roles. The public defender, the priest, the psychiatrist—all can be seen in their respective roles as rescuers.

Clutter family murders was popularized by Truman Capote's book, *In Cold Blood*. The Manson family murderers operated from a religious, sexual and drug-oriented background. Third degree losers have existed throughout history and around the world. Each third degree loser that I have known depicts a high Critical Parent and a high Adapted Child, with low Nurturing Parent, Adult, and Free Child. With this type of egogram, everyone loses. Shakespeare's portrait of Richard III is a prototype of the evil villain who, with his small stature and hunched back, felt miserable about himself and responded with murderous revenge.[13]

LIBERATED PEOPLE

Liberated people are winners—whether they are single, coupled, divorced, widowed, young, or old. They operate from an "I'm OK, you're OK" position. This is evident in the following situation.

An ambulance rushes the feverish patient to the hospital emergency room. The patient has been sick most of the day with an excruciating pain in the right lower side of his abdomen. After a thorough examination, the doctor diagnoses acute appendicitis. The patient is told, "You have a case of appendicitis, and must have your appendix removed." The loser's response is, "Oh, no! Just as things were starting to get well, this had to happen. It's really going to set me back. Yet another blow!" The winner's response is: "How long will the operation take, doctor, and how long will I have to be in the hospital? As long as it happened, I'm glad it happened quick. This way I don't have to think about it." The loser regarded his/her appendicitis as yet another of life's tragic blows. The winner saw it as an inconvenience which he/she could deal with.

This is similar with people in their coupling relationships. Problems will arise; winners accept their share of responsibility and avoid the chronic blame racket.[14] Winners accept the setbacks as inconveniences and promptly find growth-promoting solutions. The loser's approach is the opposite. He/she is frequently seen in a "poor me" state, or perhaps in an "I'm going to make those bastards pay for this" state. A TA summary of a liberated couple follows.

With winners, who are liberated people, there is growth, understanding, and support for the positive aspects in each other and themselves. They and their social contacts mutually bring out the best in each other. Their pastimes are interesting, informative, and thought-provoking. They structure their lives to achieve intimacy and creative fulfillment in their leisure time. Winners may spend time playing games, but it is not a significant part of their lives. Liberated people are not stereotyped in their behavior, and they have a genuine autonomy. Likewise, liberated people have fluctuating and varying egograms, depending on their particular situation of viable, rewarding patterns. There are, however, some universal characteristics in the egograms of winners who have coupled successfully.

1. The couples' egograms of two winners, when compared, have at least two areas of confluence. Frequently, however, they share more than two areas. They are not completely alike, as certain personality differences promote stimulating growth and challenge.
2. The Nurturing Parent, Adult, or Free Child is a required area to be shared in common. An unsuccessful couple would be characterized by their two highest areas in common being the Critical Parent and Adapted Child.
3. The Adult may or may not be high. The Adult is not a measurement of a person's IQ—it is a reflection of how frequently one is operating from an Adult egostate. Confluent Adults are a helpful but not necessary prerequisite for a winning relationship.
4. Awareness is a common quality of liberated people.
5. Change is championed over rigidity and fixation. Even though a couple may start their lives together with unproductive and unpleasant behavior, the situation can take a startlingly positive twist. This is because growth is in the protoplasm of all existence, and change is possible in every individual.

6. Risk-taking is not viewed as negative. The couple exhibiting the taking-each-other-for-granted syndrome may one day rediscover each other. This can lead to new areas of fulfillment, or they may separate and seek out other people who are compatible with their needs.

Two liberated people may get together and find that they are ineffective as a team. They may both be inherently OK people, but there are innumerable reasons why people combine or dissolve as couples. Preferences for one another may be analogous to preferences in literature. Some people enjoy an anecdote, and then move on to another quip. There are those who like short stories, while others lean toward allegories. Others again opt for a long-drawn-out novel. When an OK, liberated person who has a short-story lifestyle gets together with another who has a long-drawn-out novel style, they recognize that even though they're both OK, they are not for each other at this time. The winner accepts the other person as being different but not necessarily bad. Human beings exude highly personal tastes, and this gives some insight into those who never marry and others who never "unmarry." Every style is positive—winners recognize that other people are unique. Diversity may reign for some, while for others constancy will predominate.

When autonomous winners separate, it is done in a positive, constructive, and caring way. The experience may entail a specific period of suffering, but later they are individually off to seek new horizons. The split does not occur from a competitive standpoint, nor does it imply that one is right and the other wrong. Winners clearly recognize that there are many OK people and that others will find them OK as well.

FOOTNOTES FOR PHILOSOPHERS

1. S. Karpman, "Overlapping Egograms," *TAJ*, vol. 4, no. 4, October 1974, pp. 16–19. Comparative egograms have been researched by others. Eric Schiff, in a presentation to the 11th

ITAA Annual Summer Conference of San Francisco, 1973, in a panel entitled "Recent Advances in Egograms," has constructed a model with which he shows how mothers have overlapped in a symbiotic way with their children. Dr. John Gladfelter, Dallas, Texas, personal communication, 1974, has presented a composite egogram of different family constellations and has found that psychotherapists tend to have certain types of egograms.

2. The four classifications of positions were first discussed by E. Berne, in "Classification of Position," *TAB*, vol. 1, no. 23, July 1962. He elaborated on this in his *Principles of Group Treatment*. Berne's most recent detailed discussion appears in *What Do You Say After You Say Hello?*, pp. 85–96. T. Harris popularized this idea in *I'm OK, You're OK*. Harris, however, believed that the young child was in the "I'm Not OK" position, which made rescuing a necessity. Berne felt that children were born OK, and adverse influences contributed to later malfunctions.

3. Allen and Houston, *op. cit.* They point out that it is sometimes possible to control "acting out" behavior by telling the individual what he/she will do in advance. In the terms of TA, this exposure will hook the curiosity of the Child, who will wonder, "How does the psychiatrist know that?" and will also allow the Adult to think about the predictable patterns that he/she lives.

4. J. Dusay, "Big Mama," *TAJ*, vol. 1, no. 3, July 1971.

5. When one partner of a marital pair temporarily shifts his/her psychic energy into other areas, there are marked tendencies by the other to pull that person back into the usual pattern. It is possible that a marriage could dissolve because the partner does not view the changes positively. If the change becomes permanent, it is highly unlikely that the partner will not change also. This is why the prudent therapist offers all members of the family unit an opportunity for therapy, or at least ensures that all the members of the family are made aware that the possibility of change in psychotherapy may radically affect their lives.

6. Symbiosis, as defined by J. and A. Schiff in "Passivity," *TAJ*, vol. 1, no. 1, January, 1971, has the structure shown in Figure I-13, with the combined egostates from two individuals resulting in the structure of one total personality.

7. The Imago diagram, in Berne's *Principles of Group Treatment*, is simple and unique for each individual. It shows the degree of differentiation which they have achieved in their own mind toward other members of the group. For example, William had

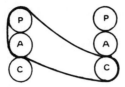

Figure I-13. Symbiosis

very little differentiation for other members of the group, who seemed to have little meaning for him (much as his own children did), but viewed the therapist as a potent, parental force (see Figure I-14):

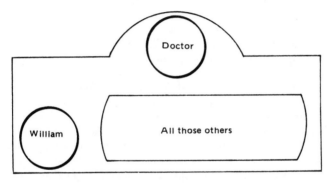

Figure I-14. A Group Imago Figure (Entering group)

8. Dr. William Masters of the famed Masters and Johnson sex research and treatment team reported at the American Psychiatric Association's 128th Annual Meeting in Anaheim, California, May 5–10, 1975, that about 10 to 15% of his patients responded positively after the receiving of information alone. Years ago, Eric Berne mentioned that a small percentage of his clients got better from simple factual information alone. The egogram does give information and also points to areas of resistance to change. The other 85% profit from attention to vital areas of resistance, illustrated by William's case.

9. The distinguishing feature between banal and tragic life scripts was reported by Steiner in *Scripts People Live.* He found that about 80% of the people have banal or uneventful types of life scripts, although they may be miserable. Another 10 to 20% have

dramatic occurrences in which bodily damage ensues—suicide, homicide, cirrhosis of the liver from drinking too much alcohol, and other such physical damage. The latter are known as tragic or *harmartic* life scripts.

10. These early messages from parents are seen as permissions to their children and life pathology is thus seen as conformity. There is probably no better illustration of this than when Bunny's father irately called her mother a whore. The little girl in her listened, believed it, and only had to figure out how to do it, which was not difficult to accomplish.

11. This is the phenomenon known as "reparenting." See J. Schiff, *All My Children,* New York: M. Evans, 1970, in which this technique has been thoroughly explored.

12. Synanon for ex-drug addicts and the Delancey Street Foundation for ex-prison inmates are two organizations that emphasize a strong family commitment. These types of rehabilitation are time- and effort-consuming, but have effective results. Less intense efforts, such as counseling and psychotherapy, are prone to failure because they are "drops in the bucket." The lay public has placed hope from time to time in the psychiatric profession in providing creative results for people with hardcore personality disorders. Unfortunately, the psychiatric profession has sometimes responded by taking on the task in a rather anemic way, and falling short as therapy fails and crimes and violence recur. See Lewis Yablonsky, *The Tunnel Back: Synanon,* New York: Macmillan, 1965.

13. An Oriental prototype of the villain is Kassaps of Sigiriya in Sri Lanka (Ceylon) (A.D. 473–491), a monstrous eccentric who committed parricide.

14. Losers like to fix the blame on their spouses and sometimes attempt to set up the marriage counselor's office like a courtroom, accusing, counter-accusing, defending, cross-examining, etc., in the hope that the therapist will judge in their favor. Sometimes they have to relentlessly pursue the search for evidence:

HUSBAND: "I called you a bitch because you came home late."
WIFE: "I came home late because you were grouchy this morning."
HUSBAND: "I was grouchy because you sulked."
WIFE: "You didn't kiss me."
HUSBAND: "You sneered."
WIFE: "You sighed."
HUSBAND: "You wrinkled your brow."
WIFE: "You twitched your cheek."

HUSBAND: "Your eyelid blinked."
WIFE: "Etc., etc."

They hone in on each other trying to prove that the other person started the argument. It becomes apparent that an electron microscope will have to be employed to see who moved what muscle first. For that reason, I, as therapist and counselor, have decided to focus only on the patterns between people, and not try to "fix" who started it.

10

Symptoms

Some people direct their conflicts toward others; other people internalize their conflicts, with specific "symptoms" ensuing. A direct, vital relationship exists between the egogram and the inner biological functioning of the body. An imbalance of the autonomic and involuntary nervous system may result in hypertension, ulcers, colitis, headaches, weight fluctuations (over and under), heart palpitations, rashes, and indigestion, to mention a few.[1] In certain individuals the external "vibrations" (egograms) have been found to be *causally* and directly related to the internal functioning. The description of Type A and Type B heart-attack proneness is a recent, well-documented example of personality type related to physical disease.[2]

Big Mama (Bertha) continued with her chronic obesity problem until she dedicated her energies to raising her Free Child and Adult egostates. There was a direct correlation between her weight reduction and her newly acquired personality strengths. Bertha's deficient Free Child was the determining factor of her overeating (see p. 169). The little girl in her was stroke-starved. Other pathological bodily symptoms develop when there is a deficiency in a particular egostate expression.

STU'S HYPERTENSION

Stu, thirty-five years old and suffering from serious high blood pressure, was referred to me by his internist. He was taking specific medications which helped somewhat but not enough, as his high blood pressure read 200/110 (a normal range is closer to 120/80). I agreed to treat him with a psychological approach in collaboration with his current medical treatment.*

Stu had a wife, four children, and a strong religious commitment; the family's main activities centered on their church. Stu fretted about incompatibilities between himself and his wife, but refused to discuss these problems openly because he feared divorce, taboo in his religion. He had a fast-moving, high-pressured job as a rising executive, and longed to escape from his work into a restful, serene environment—but his home life was anything but that. He was called upon to reprimand his subordinates at work, and his wife set him up to issue discipline to the children when he returned home in the evening. Stu did not like to say "No" and resented his role both at work and at home as a disciplinarian.

Although Stu genuinely loved and cared for his children, he felt that he had little time to express his creativity because of the many responsibilities he passively accepted. He would have temper tantrums to keep people out of his way. He would drive recklessly between home and work, clench his fists and growl at other drivers, but carefully avoid yelling obscenities. His family found him increasingly difficult to talk to, and his children offered their prayers for him during Sunday services. When Stu angrily withdrew, his wife would insult him by saying to the neighbors, "Stu's in one of his moods again." His egogram in his first TA session was that shown in Figure J-1.

Stu's outbursts resembled a rebellious little boy's tantrums. He would hold his breath until his face turned red, wave his arms, and beat the walls or the floor with his fists. An Adapted Child tantrum is generally boisterous and comes and goes quickly. As seen in his egogram, Stu's Adapted Child was very high, therefore his children were disciplined by a grown up "little boy"—which didn't work. The discipline of the Critical Parent, which is noted to be quite low in Stu, is strong, deci-

---

*Attention to both physical and psychological factors results in far more complete treatment.

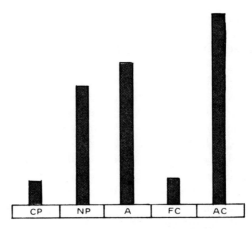

Figure J-1. Stu's "Before" Egogram

sive, and consistent—it is useful in child rearing unless, of course, it is overdone. (Stu's situation shows that Critical Parent is not totally bad and that underdevelopment can be unfortunate. Instead of setting firm limits for his children's demands, he would fight with them. Their demands were incessant because they had not learned when they pushed their father too far.)

A group member asked Stu, "Who would you like to get off your back?" Immediately, Stu lashed out at all the major women in his life: his mother, his wife, his supervisor, even his two daughters. He said that all women inhibited, berated, and limited him. He felt that he was not permitted to express creative ideas or mention anything out of the traditional, established pattern. To him, all women harbored high expectations while maintaining their critical attitudes. Stu confessed that he was both frightened of them and committed to them. He plaintively asked the group, "How do you throw out your own mother, get rid of your wife when divorce isn't possible, and then fire your boss?" Stu felt firmly locked into his difficulties.

He was encouraged to use the double chair technique, in which he talked to those fantasized, oppressive women in an empty chair. He initially experienced tremendous resistance, but then by shifting into an Adult position he was able to surface his strict training to respect women and *never* criticize. The group encouraged him to practice by telling each fantasized woman in the empty chairs what his true feelings were. They discouraged his temper tantrums, but supported astute, critical statements. As Stu's confidence grew, he began to express strong, accurate critical comments to these imaginary women. Eventually his new critical abilities solidified.

The first actual, real-life confrontation between Stu and his mother arose concerning her method of giving presents. He summoned his courage and firmly told her to desist sending his children Christmas money, insisting that he would return it to her if she disobeyed him. He took a firm Critical Parent stand on this issue instead of his usual temper tantrum. This represented an authentic shift in his psychic energy, from Adapted Child to Critical Parent. Stu felt shaky and scared at first, because this was the only time in his life in which he had stood up to his mother. She responded with a peculiar expression, and said, "Well, if you say so."

Later, he confronted his wife on an important issue and was met with a "fireworks" display. But Stu did not balk; he stood by his convictions. "Strangely," his blood pressure began going down (he carried his own measurement device at his doctor's recommendation). Stu's blood pressure remained stable at 140/90, as his Critical Parent became stronger and more assertive. He began to challenge his female boss, and actually felt stronger in standing up to her authority. She then confessed that she felt a newfound respect for him. Stu no longer directed his hostilities internally; instead, he expressed his opinions in a forthright, vibrant, positive manner. Now he did not need to sulk and throw temper tantrums, because he had effectively developed a personal protection device, known as his Critical Parent. Because Stu remained an inherently fair person, there was no concern that he would turn into a tyrant, and he actually felt his daughters respected him more. The fact that he took some risk of losing his job was overshadowed by the gains he made physiologically. Stu's "After" egogram follows (Figure J-2):

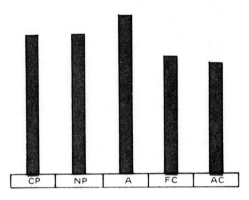

Figure J-2. Stu's "After" Egogram

Stu used his head (high Adult) to direct his authentic anger toward the source of his frustration—his mother and his wife—and decreased his childlike beatings of the children. The kids were relieved, and his wife could take care of herself; she actually appreciated having his anger "out in the open" where it could be dealt with in a straightforward manner.

ULCER TYPE I

A hard-driving executive used his logical mind to attain prominence and respect in his company. He exuded an abundance of parental qualities toward his fellow employees in that he was highly complimentary as well as critical toward their work. Unfortunately, he did not get his own personal needs met, either at home or on the job. He lamented that his sexual life was dull and infrequent. It was noticed that his ability to compromise and get along with other people was rigidly inhibited (Figure J-3).

This man had his first ulcer flare-up while working overtime. The gnawing pain in his stomach grew but he did not mention it to any of his employees or his wife. Later, the pain became quite severe and when he doubled up his wife drove him to the local hospital, despite his futile protests. He was admitted into

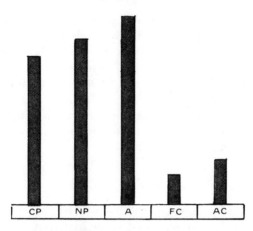

Figure J-3. Ulcer Type I

the hospital, and treated like a little boy in that he was given milky-white liquid by the nurse who administered feedings. As he swallowed the chalky white medication, he came to the startling realization that the world would go on perfectly well without him. He began resting easier after this, and actually looked forward to being cared for and fed. He experienced a new, relaxed, and cooperative demeanor. As a result of his hospitalization his ulcer cleared up rapidly, while his egogram also underwent a big shift (see Figure J-4):

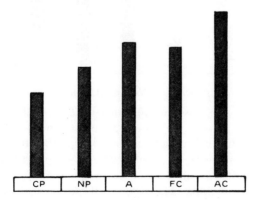

Figure J-4. Ulcer Type I's Egogram During Treatment

Although hospitalization was a temporary respite, this illustrates that his Adapted Child was effectively raised. In this milieu he was able to *accept* authentic strokes and nurturing from others. In this way, he didn't have to "eat out" his stomach to compensate. His Free Child became strengthened in the process, and his ulcer healed as he appreciated the chance to feel good in a "give-and-take" manner. Following hospitalization psychological treatment was commenced to bring about a lasting shift in his personality.

ULCER TYPE II

Another ulcer patient in the hospital had an egogram which was remarkably similar to that of the hypertensive Stu. He was incredibly angry and completely unwilling to express it (see Figure J-5):

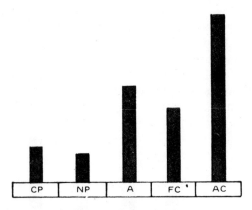

Figure J-5. Ulcer Type II Egogram

He harbored a deep-seated resentment toward his mother and all women in general. He would set up ingenious situations in which he would be guaranteed an insult, retort, or even physical abuse. On buses, he would race old or pregnant ladies to the last vacant seat, gleefully win, and then get yelled at by an indignant bystander. Throughout these typical scenes, his stomach quietly churned away. He utilized his uncanny ability for making women angry—from the waitress to the grocery clerk. His atrocious behavior ensured that no one (including himself) would be able to stand up for him and be on his side.

In his psychotherapy group, he had every female member "on his back." His obvious "Kick Me" game was identified in the first ten minutes, and the group agreed to the proposal that he be deprived of his usual, negative "Kick me" strokes. They wouldn't support his game. He went through the usual curative steps of redecision, practice, and resistance-avoidance, and then he became warm and complimentary toward women. He became accepted and noticed that his gastrointestinal complaints began to vanish at the same time that his external psychological behavior changed.

These different ulcer examples illustrate that people with specific symptoms do not necessarily have similar egograms; however, it has been consistently shown that relief from the physical symptom of psychosomatic problems is accompanied by an egogram *shift* in energy.

Specific symptoms are directly related to an individual's unique script or life plan. A curious finding appears when an individual is asked to remember what was his/her favorite room as he/she was growing up. Some recall the dining room or kitchen; others the bathroom, bedroom, or living room; while others lean toward the closet or even the garage. Symptomology seems to revolve around specific rooms in houses and to correspond with physiological body areas. Each family seems to emphasize different body areas, organs, orifices, and sphincters; later in life different people nostalgically recall certain rooms as being more important. Lasting decisions occur in specific rooms which vary according to families. Let me illustrate this by the example of a bathroom type of family. A little boy brought home a bad report card and his worried mother asked, "Did you drink your prune juice today?" This mother knew that prune juice in the morning causes a trip to the bathroom at least once a day. Her belief, passed down to her by her own mother, was that a bowel movement a day has a beneficial effect upon intelligence.

The little boy had been programmed by his mother to worry about his bowels. When things went right, he attributed it to regularity; when things went wrong, he first suspected that it was because of improper elimination. This shows up in the development of his egogram later in life, which will be a high Adapted Child if he "tried" hard to conform; a high Critical Parent if he is irritated about irregularity in others; a high Adult for parisitologists; a high Nurturing Parent for healers (of bowel problems); and a high Free Child for some abstract artists who smear heavy oils.[3]

Kitchen families make their important decisions in that room and frequently have stomach or eating problems. Dining room types are similar to kitchen people, but more formal. Living room people are frequently social; they talk and sigh a great deal, and take a lot of air in and out of their lungs. Bedroom families stress sex. And so it goes on. Of course, combinations exist to color the personalities, and the expression of egostates is influenced by the underlying orifices.

A specific egogram does not reveal a particular psychosomatic problem; that is early life programming. But egograms do aid in shifting psychic energy from one egostate to another. The shift is more important for lasting results than the treatment of a specific symptom.

FOOTNOTES FOR PHILOSOPHERS

1. Reading the label on a patent medicine bottle reveals how long the list of physical symptoms that are related to problems of psychological living can be. Fiction writiers correlate personality types with body symptoms (i.e., Falstaff and obesity, Dr. Zhivago and heart attack). Dr. Flanders Dunbar and other pioneers in the field of psychosomatic medicine have related most known bodily ills to personality traits. Many of Dr. Dunbar's conclusions have been refuted; however, some of her observations remain solid. F.

Dunbar, *Emotion and Bodily Changes,* 4th edition, New York: Columbia University Press, 1954.

2.   M. Friedman and H. Rosenman, *Type A Behavior and Your Heart,* New York: Knopf, 1974. This correlates certain "hurry up" types of people with a higher risk of coronary disease. T. Kahler, and H. Capers in "The Miniscript," *TAJ,* vol. 45, no. 1, 1974, show how certain people are driven by "hurry up" messages from parents in early life which show up in their day-to-day happenings.

3.   Eric Berne observed that there must be a lot of bathroom families, witnessed by the large number of colonic irrigation parlors listed in the yellow pages of the telephone directory in any metropolis.

11

Authority Conflicts

Lucifer was well known as a "little devil" and a "hell raiser." At the time of his first haircut, the gentle barber finally surrendered and closed his shop for the day when Lucifer picked up the aerosol shaving cans and wrote his name on the mirror, two chairs, and the cash register. In the barber's conceding speech, he told Lucifer's mother that she might try buying a do-it-yourself haircutting kit for future haircuts. At the age of three, Lucifer's life script was emerging. He continually challenged all established authorities, beginning with the barbershop. He created scenes when he discovered other's vulnerable spots, and on every occasion during his youth, he was *sent home* to his mother.

Lucifer was considered to be too "immature" for nursery school. Later, during his first Boy Scout outing, his parents were frantically summoned to pick him up from the local Boy Scout camp. He had received his final warning for the disappearance of the ice cream from the camp kitchen, many of the tents were falling down, and there was also the matter of the garter snakes in the camp director's sleeping bag.

Lucifer's habitual, colorful history of being expelled and banned from social functions was no mystery. It adhered to the same pattern which eventually developed into the *expectations* of others. Fifteen years earlier in the barbershop, Lucifer's

194

behavior was not fully habitual; it was in its fledgling state of development. By the time he reached high school, the pattern was set, and he was notorious for being uncontrollable. In his senior yearbook, a classmate pegged him with the expression: "A success at failure." The community, as well as the school, *expected* him to be the way he was and treated him in a stereotyped manner.

Lucifer's mother played helpless when it came to disciplining him. Whenever she said a harsh word, she would sheepishly withdraw, then make it up to him by presenting him with a beautiful dinner or a piece of pie. Father rarely disciplined because it interfered with his own drinking pattern. When Lucifer's father gulped down the alcoholic elixir, he explained that it was done to calm his nerves. Lucifer was frequently treated to the spectacle of his father being carted home by pub-crawling friends.

Lucifer performed well on his college entrance exams and entered the state university. However, his academic potential went unfulfilled because he repeated his usual "dropout" pattern. He remained at college for nearly a semester, but when it was time to take his final examinations, two major events occurred. First, his roommate kicked him out because of the loud blasting of his stereo; second, he was introduced to a psychedelic drug by a friend majoring in chemistry. The concoction relieved his anxiety about taking the finals—he slept through all five of them. When his college counselor received word that he had missed his finals, Lucifer was called in for an interview. He appeared late, disheveled, and disoriented. The counselor immediately contacted the school's health services. After Lucifer had spent a chaotic month in the mental health ward, the staff concluded that he would not be able to measure up to the college's standards. He was referred back to his sympathetic parents, who gratefully drove him home, as they had periodically done in the past.

Mother's response was consistent with those that she had given him since his first haircut. She lightly chided him, insinuated that he was turning out to be just like his father, and then asked if he wanted ice cream on the pie she had just baked for him. His arrival resembled a gala occasion, and his mother nearly outdid herself with his homecoming meal. Even his father poured himself a few extra drinks for the occasion.

Lucifer's college counselor wrote the family a letter recommending a course of psychotherapy for both Lucifer and his parents. Lucifer went to the local psychiatric clinic for an evaluation and a work-up. Before his visit, he took some more LSD and was consequently inarticulate and "spaced out" during his interview. The psychiatrist recommended that he remain at the hospital under constant observation. After a closely supervised week, his parents were called in for a three-way interview.

At the meeting, Lucifer's mother appealed to the psychiatrist by saying, "I've always wanted the best for Lucifer. I wanted him to go to school, learn a profession, get married and have children. We've always done everything we could to help." A curious expression flashed across Lucifer's face, which implied that this was not a straight message. The psychiatrist, acknowledging the look on Lucifer's face, asked him when he had felt this way before. Lucifer insightfully recalled a departure scene which he labeled as a most important event. It occurred when he was ready to leave for college, as his parents drove him to the train station to see him off. Mother had baked him a batch of cookies to take with him. Just as the whistle from the approaching train sounded, his mother got a pained expression on her face and clutched at her heart. Lucifer became morose and confused; he decided that he couldn't leave for college that day. When he finally left for school a week later, his mother took him aside and said, "Son, I know you'll do well in college. Everything will be all right—Gulp!" This one little "gulp" overshadowed all the other messages which implied that he would be bright and successful, and it negated all the inspiration she had attempted to instill in him. When confronted with this recollection of her gulp, Mother chided, "That's silly, dear. I've always wanted what is best for you." Lucifer's father interrupted at this point by saying that Mother never wanted Lucifer to go to college, the Boy Scout camp, or even to leave home under any circumstances. Father confirmed the fact that she would get upset and nervous when it came time for Lucifer to go anywhere. On a hidden level, Mother clearly did not want to lose her only son. The incidents compelling Lucifer to fail at goals and then return home began to add up. Lucifer's passive father recounted these situations with bleary eyes, then excused himself from the setting, presumably to get another drink. Lucifer's script matrix then looked like this (Figure K-1):

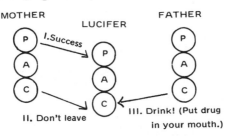

Figure K-1. Lucifer's Script Matrix

The script matrix visually depicts the essential transactions which comprise a life script.[1] The mother's Parent egostate gives the "success" value (I). On the surface, she sent him to the barbershop so that he could get a haircut like the other big boys. She sent him to the Cub and Boy Scout camp, and to various fine schools. It looked as if she wanted him to succeed. However, the little-girl part (Child egostate) of Mother was frightened and reluctant to see him leave. She gave him a hidden curse, or injunction (II), which was "Gulp! Don't leave." She had been given an identical injunction by her own father when she was growing up, and she "inadvertently" passed it on to Lucifer, like a hot potato.[2] Lucifer unwaveringly *conformed* to these hidden messages. He continually botched his endeavors, and was sent home. Difficult as it is to live with two incompatible messages saying, "Go and be successful," and "Don't leave," Lucifer looked to his father for a resolution. Somehow his father had succeeded in living with his mother for over twenty-five years by getting drunk and being passive. These were Father's tools, which Lucifer used in the "here's how" message (III) (see Figure K-1, Lucifer's Script Matrix). Lucifer resolved his dilemma with a more modern approach—

LSD. His mental trips guaranteed that he would be sent home to the safety of Mother's nest.

Lucifer may be termed "rebellious" because he would not comply with his mother's "success" messages. However, the term "pseudo-rebel" is more appropriate because he actually *conformed* with his mother's hidden, potent injunction: "Don't leave." Authentic rebellion does not conform with any script message.

AUTHENTIC REBEL

The human body has an amazing ability to take punishment and then restore itself. The human psyche has the same potential. At this point, the therapist introduced Mother, Father, and Lucifer to the concepts of psychic energy and egograms. The family constructed their own egograms, and they came out like this (Figures K-2, K-3, and K-4):

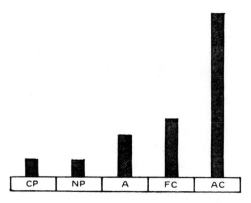

Figure K-2. Lucifer's Father

The egograms intrigued them, and they busily began using their Adult egostates to analyze what they meant. Mother wanted to raise her Free Child so that she could become carefree and have some fun. Father opted to raise his Parent parts, so that he could escape from his perpetual position of "houseboy." Lucifer decided to raise both his Adult and his Parent egostates. He admitted that the first way to begin was by

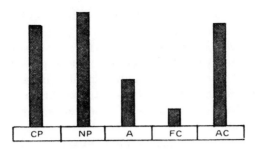

Figure K-3. Lucifer's Mother

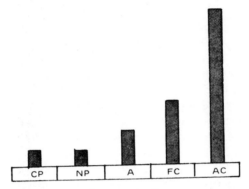

Figure K-4. Lucifer

giving up LSD. The family members now had a tool with which to get a fresh look at themselves and others, and to appreciate the strengths and weaknesses of each other. The family symbiosis (cf. p. 180) began to dissolve. The egogram analysis pointed clearly to the avenues of change. They then utilized the principles of change (Chapter Six), took an action which was an alternative to their usual style, recognized and overcame resistances with the aid of the therapist, and finally practiced the newfound personality strengths until they became incorporated and felt natural.

Mother strengthened her deficient egostate parts, which allowed her to achieve autonomy and to live without her son. One of the nice things about egograms is that attention can be focused on Mother's own personality and she too can be seen as a complex human being. Unfortunately, a great deal of energy has been drained by mental health professionals in rescuing "poor" children from their "malicious" mothers. At one time it seemed that the psychiatric journals ascribed everything from homosexuality to halitosis to "evil" mothers. Sometimes it seems that the world has forgotten that mothers are people too. In this case, the best course is to view the mother's total personality, not as an object of wrath but for its growth potential. Lucifer acquired enough Adult and Parent to take care of himself completely. Father cut down on his drinking and actively stated his opinions.

Occasionally, pseudo-rebels play their games with substitute persons, like parole officers and social workers, rather than actual family members. A pseudo-rebel operates from a high Adapted Child position and conforms to a hidden message, which may appear to be antithetical to the stated position.

An "authentic rebel" is distinguished from the pseudo-rebel because he/she does not comply with a "Don't leave" injunction. The authentic rebel has very little Adapted Child in relation to his or her other egostates. A true rebellion occurs when the individual incorporates a strong Adult with a powerful Free Child. (These are also recognized as the necessary ingredients for creativity. This explains why successful revolutions are unique; they are not copies of somebody else's old revolution.) The goal of an authentic rebel is change; the goal of a pseudo-rebel conforms to a hidden script message. With authentic rebellion there is a possibility of failure and the rebel may suffer alienation from his or her family, ostracism socially, and exile or death in the political realm. However, the true rebel will accept reasonable risk in order to gain his or her personal freedom.

Throughout this book, episodes from my clinical practice have been presented. In this and the three preceding chapters the most commonly occurring human concerns of loneliness, conflict in marriage and coupling, the turning of psychological hurts against one's own body, and authority conflicts have been presented in detail. It can be seen that authentic rebellion is the key to growth and change in all these situations.

Lucifer's pseudo-rebellion was superficial, like flailing his head against a brick wall; in actuality he had no rebellion at all, only a conformity to negative influences and injunctions from his parents. Authentic rebellion is accomplished by clear recognition, distinction, and creative action. The ability to recognize destructive influences passed down from one's ancestors, and the willingness to sort out and distinguish the positive messages from the negative, is the prerequisite for release from psychological slavery. If we can stand back and watch ourselves transact with other people—while remaining willing to interrupt ulterior "game"-type transactions—we can avoid stumbling through life in a stereotyped, habitual way, causing misery to ourselves and others.

FOOTNOTES FOR PHILOSOPHERS

1. See the important script books, E. Berne, *What Do You Say After You Say Hello?*, and C. Steiner, *Scripts People Live.*
2. The "Hot Potato" phenomenon was described by F. English in her article "Episcript and the Hot Potato Game," *TAB*, 8:77-82, Oct., 1969. In this situation, the injunction part of the script is passed on like a hot potato by the childlike or archaic elements of the parent. It is surmised that Lucifer's mother had been told by her own father when she was a little girl that in some way she was not OK, and that what she did would not turn out all right, including her rearing of her own children. In turn, grandfather's injunction came from his mother, Lucifer's great grandmother. By the time we find where the hot potato originates, we've slipped further back than the Civil War and may end up on Mt. Olympus while Zeus reigned. Actually, there have only been about two hundred script passages (or generations) since the golden age of Greece, but it seems rather silly to blame Greek ancestors for present-day problems.

   Script injunctions may relate to early cultural prototypes and be expressed in the mythology of the civilization; the replay comes through folk tales, fairy tales, etc. Those clinicians following the theories of Carl Jung, with his emphasis on the collective unconscious, find much evidence of the reflection of mythological characters in the present-day personalities of their clients. Transactional analysts likewise find this, but emphasize that the transmission is by direct mother/father transactions from their Child egostates, to their offspring. Rather than focus upon a *mystical* or *unconscious* replay, it happens by words and gestures at beddy-bye time.

THE CHOICE IS YOURS

The five principal passions which unfold in everyday life—and consequently in my consulting room—are criticism, nurturing, reason, freedom, and adaptation. These passions may make either a positive or a negative appearance when they operate in each person as a function of his or her egostates. Some people are reasonably content with the amount and balance of energies in their various egostates, and when specific conflicts arise, they are able to handle them comfortably. Others are less content.

In recent years, I have found that the egogram is as reliable a tool as has yet been devised for promoting individual responsibility. It does not purport to be the "true meaning of life," nor is it offered as a chariot of transcendence into higher levels of consciousness. Rather, the egogram is a portrait of the personality which illustrates both the intensity of human passions and the balance between these forces—forces well within our power to control. With it, we are now able to see *how* we are; and, if we so choose, to do something about what we see.

SUBJECT INDEX

Adapted Child
  advantages of, 116
  cautions in using, 118
  compliant pseudo-rebellious, 52
  definition of, 4
  disadvantages of, 116
  resistances to raising, 118
  sample of egograms, 45–47
  techniques in raising, 116–118
Adult
  advantages of, 106
  cautions in using, 110
  definition of, xv, 4
  disadvantages of, 106
  resistances to raising, 110
  sample of egograms, 40–42
  techniques for raising, 107–110
Alcohol, window-shade effect of
    upon egostate energy, 127–128
Amphetamines, effect of usage upon
    egostate energy, 128

Body language, observance of in
    discerning egostates, 22, 33

Confrontation, 99
Constancy Hypothesis
  definition of, 122–123
  summary of, 131–132
"Cosmic whistle", definition of, 120

Creativity
  effect of emotional life/
    relationships upon, 153
  union of feeling and thinking in,
    xxiii
Critical Parent
  advantages of, 113
  cautions in using, 115–116
  definition of, 3
  disadvantages of, 114
  resistances to raising, 115
  sample of egograms, 35–37
  techniques in raising, 114–115

Delancey Street Foundation, 182
Depression, description of, 130–131
Double chair
  to overcome impasse (slippage), 89
  for redecision, 88
  for role playing and experiencing
    prototype episode, 83–84
  use of
    in curing hypertensive person,
      186–187
    in raising Critical Parent, 114
Dreams
  deprivation of, 134–135
  Fritz Perls' work in, 98
  in representing only one aspect of
    personality, 69

Egogram
  age of subjects in validity of, 69–70
  consensual validation of, 59
  construction of, 17–18
  couples' egograms, 71, 77–78, 155
  definition of, ix, xv, 3
  development of, 12
  equivalent of psychological
      fingerprints, 35
  false positives, 63–65
  group egograms, 74–75
  as tool for change, growth, xxiii
  interference, 63
  reliability of, 59–60
  shift in, as indication of growth, 76,
      101, 191
  summary of, 203
  third party egogram, 68
  use of intuition in constructing, 18
Egostate
  as active determinants, xvi
  definition of, xvi
  definition of Child, Adult and
      Parent egostates, xv
  egostate energy, xx–xxi
Empathy, 117
Encounter groups, 11
  casualties of, xx, 152
  success of, explained by Constancy
      Hypothesis, 132
Endogram concept, 77
Eric Berne Seminar of San Francisco,
      xxiii, 33, 59, 77–78, 133
Esalen, xi, xx

Free Child
  advantages of, 102
  cautions in using, 106
  definition of, 4
  disadvantages of, 102
  resistances to raising, 105–106
  sample of egograms, 42–45
  techniques in raising, 103–104
Frigidity, 160

Games
  definition of, xvii
  "Blemish—Hee, Hee", 145
  as common sexual game, 10, 11
  "Criticize me", 160
  "Do Me Something", 164
  "Kick Me", xviii, 70
  "Marshmallow Throwing", 62
  "Now I got You, You S.O.B.", 70,
      149, 158
  "Psychiatry", 61–62
  "Rapo", 22–23
  "Rescue Me", 160
  "Stupid", 15, 61
  "Tease", 142–143
Gestalt, xxi
  blending with TA, xxiv
Goddess Kali, 133
Growth, potential for, xiii, xv
Growth model
  definition of, 132
  compared to medical model, 132
  "Here and Now", xxiii

Heroes, 73
Heroin
  effect of usage upon egostate
      energy, 126–127
  as substitute for "mother's milk",
      134
Homeostasis, 133
"Hooking", definition of, 28
"Hot potato", description of
      phenomenon, 201
Hugging, response to in egostate
      identification, 25
Hypertension, 184
Hypochondria, 81–86

Imago (diagram), 180–181
Impasse, functional, 90
  structural definition of, by
      Goulding, 99–100
Interpretation, anticipatory, 153, 180

Intuition
definition of, xxiv, 5
Eric Berne's studies on, 98

Krishna, 119

"Liberated people"
various types of, 179
as winners, 177
Loneliness, 139
Losers, 176–177, 182
LSD, 195, 196

Mania, 129–130
"Martian", 107, 131-132
Medical model, 132
Miniscript, driver, 56, 201
"Mother's milk", 125–129, 134

Nurturing Parent
advantages of, 110–111
cautions in using, 113
definition of, 4
disadvantages of, 111
resistances to raising, 112
sample of egograms, 37–40
techniques for raising, 111–112

Obesity, 166
Orgasm, 9
Overprescribing, 96

Pastime, example of a, 158
Permission, 119
Permission groups, xx
Pheromones, 27, 34
Potency, 119
Practice, 92–93
Protection, 119
Prototype episode, 84
compared to Freud's hyperesthetic
memory, 98
Psyche, xxiv
Psychodrama, xxi, 98

Psychogram, 65, 76–77
Psychosis, 50
Psychotherapy, group, 98
advantages of, 120

Racket
chronic blame, 177
definition of, 84
overnurturing, 108
Rebellion, 54
definition of authentic/
pseudo, 198, 201
Redecision
Mary and Robert Goulding's use
of, 98
use of, in changing scripted
personality traits, 86–88
Relationships, types of, 156
Reparenting, 176, 182
Resistances
cultural, 96–97
definition of, 102
institutional, 95–96
social, 94–95
Rinencephalon, 27
Role playing, 83
Roles, psychological, 176
Rolfing, 33

San Francisco Transactional Analysis
Seminar, x, xxi, 59, 120, 134
Schizophrenia, 76
Scripts
analysis, xx
banal, 181
harmartic, 182
injunction, 100, 201
counter-injunction, 100
life, xviii, xxiv
matrix, xix, 197
Slippage, 89–92
Strokes, xviii, xxiii, 38
Surfacing, 84
Symbiosis, 72, 180
Synanon, xx, 182

Techne, xxiv
Therapies, experiential, xx
Timing, of interventions, 142, 152
Transactional analysis
  development of, xvii
  three basic components of,
    137–138
Treatment contract
  comparison with legal contracts,
    32 fn.
  definition of, 20
Transactions, xvii

Ulcer types, composite of, 188,
    189–191
Unconscious, belief in not necessary
    for TA, xxiii, 98

"Vibrations", xv, 8

Winners
  definition of, 177
  characteristics of, 178

NAME INDEX

Abraham, Karl, 33
Allen, David, 153, 180
Anastasia, Anne, 56, 120, 153
Arguelles, Jose, xxiv

Berne, Eric, x, xv, xvi, xvii, xviii, xxi,
    xxiii, xxiv, 34, 57, 76, 98, 119, 134,
    153, 180-181, 193
Bonsall, R., 34
Boulton, Mary, x
Bruener, J. S., 100

Campbell, Joseph, xi, 73, 133
Cannon, W. B., 133
Cantlon, Marie, xi
Capers, Hedges, 56, 193, 201
Capote, Truman, 177
Chodoff, Paul, 57
Comfort, Alex, 34
Crossman, Patricia, 16
Cunningham, Glenn, xiii–xiv

David, George, x
Davis, F., 34
Del Casale, Francisco, x, 76, 77
Dement, William, 134-135
Dunbar, Flanders, 192-193
Dusay, John M., 32, 77-78, 120, 180
Dusay, Katherine, xi, 33, 57

Ellis, Havelock, 56, 153
English, Fanita, 201
Ernst, Franklin, x, 33, 120

Federn, Paul, 77
Frankel, Victor, 134
Freud, Sigmund, xvi, xvii, xxi, xxiv,
    15, 59, 98, 99, 153
Friedman, Meyer, 193

Gatz, Arthur, 34
Gladfelter, John, 180
Goulding, Mary and Robert, x, 98
Goulding, Robert, xxiv, 87, 99-100

Harlow, Harry, xxiii
Harris, Thomas, xxiii, 180
Haskell, Martin and Rochelle, xi
Hinesley, Kent, x
Houston, M., 153, 180
Humphrey, F., 135
Hurley, J., 76

James, Muriel, xxiii
Jongeward, Dorothy, xxiii
Jung, Carl, xvi, 201

Kahler, Taibi, 56, 193, 201
Kales, A., 135

Kales, J., 135
Kandathil, George, xi
Kaplan, H., 98
Karpman, Stephen, x, 71, 77–78, 154, 179
Kassaps of Sigiriya Sri Lanka (Ceylon), 182
Kendra, John, x, 56-57
Krumland, Carole, xi
Kubie, Lawrence, 133

Lawrence, D. H., 153
Leboyer, Frederick, 33
Lieberman, Morton, 152
Lorenz, Konrad, 26, 34
Lowen, Alexander, 33
Lyons, H., 57

Manson family, 177
Masters, William, 15, 181
May, Rollo, xi
Menninger, Karl, 152
Michale, R., 34
Moreno, Jacob, xi, 98

Ornstein, Robert, xxiv

Patrousky, B., 34
Perls, Fritz, xi, xxi–xxii, 98, 99
Piaget, Jean, 77
Porter, H., 76

Reich, Wilhelm, 33
Reik, Theodore, 120
Ricca, Bobbi, xi
Richard (The Third), 177
Rissman, Arthur, 77

Rolf, Ida, 33
Rosenman, Ray H., 193
Russell, Bertrand, 57

Sadock, Benjamin, 98
Satir, Virginia, xx
Schiff, Eric, 72, 78, 179–180
Schiff, Jacqui, x, xxiv, 180, 182
Shakespeare, William, 153, 177
Silverstein, Bob, xi
Singh, Jaswant, xi
Sophocles, 153
Spitz, Rene, xxiii
Stachey, J., 15
Steinberg, J., 152
Steiner, Claude, x, xix, xxiii, 32, 100, 181–182
Sullivan, Harry Stack, 24

Taylor, Rattray, 133
Thiel, Peggy, xi
Thomas, Louis, 34
Thomson, George, 58, 76
Thurber, James, 103
Tissot, Rene, 135

Van Gogh, Vincent, 56

Welch, Saroj and Carlos, xi
Wichman, Scott, 78
William of Occam, 52

Yablonsky, Lewis, 182
Yalom, Irving, 152

Zimmer, Heinrich, 119, 133, 134

DATE DUE		